240987

A FEW BLOCKS
FROM BROADWAY

A FEW BLOCKS FROM BROADWAY

Roger Royle

Hodder & Stoughton

LONDON SYDNEY AUCKLAND TORONTO

British Library Cataloguing in Publication Data

Royle, Roger
   A few blocks from Broadway.
   1. Christian life
   I. Title
   248.4   BV4501.2

ISBN 0 340 41062 0

To the memory of my Mother

ACKNOWLEDGMENTS

As with any book of this sort, it is impossible to include the names of all those people who have shown me love and helped me in both my life and my ministry. But my thanks are no less sincere. And I hope that those who are mentioned do not regret being associated with me.

Writing this book has been a great act of discipline for me. It would never have been started had I not been encouraged by June Hall and David Wavre. And it certainly would never have been completed had it not been for the typing skills of Barbara Carthew and Hilary Hunt's dedicated reading of the proofs. To Hilary and Barbara I am especially grateful, as I am to Father Tom Summers for casting an ecclesiastical eye over the script.

Thank you for taking the trouble to read it. I hope that amongst the stories, you will find an idea of God which will strengthen your own faith.

CONTENTS

1. When I was a child   9

2. I put away childish things   20

3. Fishers of men   33

4. The harvest is ready   47

5. To the ends of the earth   60

6. Except the Lord build the house   73

7. The words will be given you   87

8. Even Solomon in all his glory   100

9. Suffer the little children   113

10. Through a glass, darkly   126

11. What I have written   137

12. Take my yoke   149

1

WHEN I WAS A CHILD

To me, Broadway was a very busy street in Cardiff which I had to cross four times every Sunday on my way to and from St German's Church. As a child any thought that there was another Broadway never crossed my mind. In 1978, however, I found myself only minutes from the Broadway of the bright lights and stars.

I had been invited to preach at New York's most fashionable Episcopalian church, the one in which Andrew Lloyd-Webber decided to première his *Requiem*, St Thomas's on Fifth Avenue. It was the first Sunday after the Epiphany, and St Thomas's was coming to the end of its Christmas carol season. I decided to use one of my favourite stories, one which I had heard told years ago by a Nigerian priest. It was about a Sunday School teacher in England who was finding it difficult to keep the attention of her Sunday School class. Teaching in any school, as I was to find out some years after hearing this story, is difficult, but at times in a Sunday School it is well nigh impossible. The age range of your class can be from three-and-a-half to nine, and many teachers feel frustrated that the majority of their time has to be taken up in admiring someone's new clothes, someone else's new doll, and hearing of yet another person's grandma whose budgie has recently died. This teacher was determined that in the half-hour she had she would teach the faith. So she said to her children that she wanted them, the next week, to bring something which would represent a saying from the Bible. This, she thought, was bound to make her class come alive in a relevant and meaningful way. When the next Sunday arrived admittedly only three children had remembered. The first one was a sweet little girl who was hugging a toy lamb which had a slit in its middle out of which her nightie was hanging. When the teacher asked her which story she represented, she said, 'I am the good shepherd.' 'Marvellous,' said the teacher, 'have a packet of Smarties.' The next child was a bright little boy called Julian who was holding a candle: the flame was going up, the front of his hair was getting singed, there was wax going on the floor and the verger was going a whiter shade of pale. When Julian was asked which story he represented, he said, 'I am the light of the world.' 'Brilliant,' said the teacher, 'very well thought out, have a packet of Space Dust.' Julian went away very contented indeed. The third child was called Desmond. Now Desmond, not to put too fine a point on it, was not very bright, but he had remembered what he had been asked to do and he stood there in front of the whole class holding a lollipop. The teacher was baffled as to where lollipops were mentioned in the Bible. She thought, possibly, there was some mention of them in the Apocrypha; but she, like many of us, was weak on her Apocrypha. So she turned to Desmond and said, 'Which story from the Bible do you represent?' Desmond stood firmly, clutching his lollipop, and said in very clear terms, 'Hold fast to that which is good.' There was a spontaneous burst of laughter from the congregation, and even applause, which in those days was very rare in church. I knew that I'd got them, and in a moment of self-delight thought, 'Roger, you are only a few blocks from Broadway.' To some this would be blasphemy, but to me it was very natural. Throughout my life the church and the theatre have always gone hand in hand, but I have to confess there have been times when one has overtaken the other.

St German's was a very theatrical church. It was high Anglo-Catholic; well up the 'candle'. The altar was set at the top of a great flight of steps, and the vestments worn by the priests would rival the costumes of many a West End show. The movement of the clergy and servers showed the handi-work of a very caring, if demanding, choreographer. I had worshipped at St German's for as long as I could remember. My father had been the vicar of the next-door parish, St

Saviour's, Splott, which was equally high, but he died when I was one year old and so my mother had had to move out of the vicarage and away from the parish, but she still wanted to worship God in the way she was used to. For her to continue to worship at her husband's former church would not have been done, so she moved her allegiance to St German's but she was determined that my brother and I would be brought up, at least spiritually, in the way my father would have wanted. Certainly he would have wanted us to take a full part in worship.

At a very early age I became a boat boy, the boy who carries the incense. I was trained how to walk and not to sway like a drunken sailor; I was taught to keep my hands clasped around the incense boat and to look straight ahead. The speed at which I walked was controlled by the thurifer's hand on my shoulder. I soon realised that this part of being a boat boy called for a good sense of theatre. It was not long before I was allowed to appear on the more significant Sundays, other than the sixteenth after Trinity, or the third in Lent. I found myself being kept for the major festivals. In a cassock and a cotta that was more lace than linen, I looked angelic. I also learnt at a very early age that when you are off stage you keep quiet, so I was even held in high regard in the vestry – not an easy thing to achieve. One Christmas Eve I realised that I had hit the big time. I was put down on the rota as the boat boy for the Midnight Mass. The service was ticket only, to avoid drunks disturbing and disrupting this most beautiful service. We arrived in church very early as we were dependent on the last bus and the No 24 wasn't geared to late-night worship.

The church was packed, the music was grand and the sermon was long. It reached its climax with a procession to the crib. The vicar carried the model of the baby Jesus on a cushion and at the head of the procession was the thurifer and, of course, the boat boy. As the babe was put in the crib, Christmas really started for me. As a family we did not anticipate the feast, which might have been because we always did everything at the last minute.

After the service we were faced with the long walk home

and only when I got home and was allowed to empty my stocking did I start to complain about my feet; they were really killing me. Possibly the fact that I had my shoes on the wrong feet had something to do with the pain, but no one in church would have guessed that beneath that cherubic face there had been a slight technical hitch.

When I outgrew the lace cotta I became a choirboy. The money was good because not only were you paid once a quarter but you also had the same amount banked for you as a golden handshake when your voice broke. In that choir there was no such thing as voluntary redundancy. The quarterly pay-packet was eagerly awaited and plans of how it was going to be spent were more elaborate than any government finance bill. The spring quarter was the best paid, not just because of the extra services at Easter but also because of those Easter brides. As far as we were concerned, couples who asked for the choir at their wedding were off to a very good start.

With my first choir pay, which, if I remember correctly, was the equivalent of seven-and-a-half pence, I bought a polyanthus plant for my father's grave. As I was so young when my father died all my memories of him are second-hand. He died suddenly on Palm Sunday, so my mother was faced with having to get out of the vicarage where we lived, find a home, find a job and make sure that my brother Peter – who is three-and-a-half years my senior – and I were looked after properly. Mummy went back to teaching, first of all at St Mary's School, Bute Street in Cardiff's Tiger Bay; and Mary, who was a young girl parishioner, came to live with us so that while Mummy was at work there was always someone at home. Mary, whom we called Nanny, became part of the family and lived with us until Mummy died in 1957.

Visits to my father's grave were regular. He is buried just near Llandaff Cathedral and very sensibly my mother always referred to the grave as 'Daddy's Garden'. It was a place of hope, and visits to it were always made enjoyable. After tidying the grave we had tea in the cathedral cafe at the top of the hill which to my delight served Kunzle cakes. So despite the sadness there was always fun, but I did notice that my

'Any chance of a first aid badge?'

mother never left the graveside without saying a silent prayer.

I did not have great success in the choir, partly because my brother had a very beautiful voice and I had a tendency to sing flat, but then I am a great believer that comparisons are odious. However, my need for a sense of theatre within worship was satisfied once again when I became a server. Here once more was the opportunity to shine as a performer, but the 'run' was limited to say the least. It was not long before I went away to school and so it was only at holiday times that I was able to serve – and then only at eight o'clocks and weekday communions, services which could hardly be regarded as peak viewing.

The other outlet for my acting talent was the Cubs. My mother was a very keen Guide, it was part of her life. Friday nights were guarded for Guiding and nothing took precedence. It also meant the Guides visited our home, generally to take their cook's badge. This, to say the least, was a mixed blessing. The cooking was never elaborate and at times was decidedly dangerous. I have experienced rock cakes which, if they were dropped, would have registered highly on the Richter scale.

Peter was a keen Scout, tying knots, putting up tents, and lighting fires was his forte, but I have always liked my home comforts and the adventurous spirit which is an essential part of the Baden-Powell movement did not hold a great appeal. There was, however, one thing that did appeal and that was the annual Cub pantomime. I was willing to surrender to Grand Howls, woggles and Arkelas to be in the pantomime. My patience was rewarded; I was cast as the princess in *Hickory-Dickory-Dock*. The critics raved, and how it isn't still running I shall never know, but I am afraid that once the lights went out and the make-up was removed my enthusiasm for Cubs waned. I did make it into Scouts, but only just, and it didn't last.

My love of pantomime has never died. Each year, for as far back as I can remember, we went as a family to the pantomime at the New Theatre, Cardiff. It was an essential part of our Christmas celebrations and generally took place on 6 January, the Feast of the Epiphany, Twelfth Night. The moment the overture began I was transported into another world and as the curtain rose on the first scene, which was always the village square, I looked carefully to see if the lady with the peroxide-blonde hair who served on the egg-stall in the market was in the chorus. If she was, then I knew everything would be all right. The scenery, the costumes, the music, the acting, were all larger than life and although I may have been sitting in the stalls my heart was there, centre stage. I just waited for that one moment when heart and body would be united in the singing of the pantomime song. I always hoped that I would be sitting towards the end of a row so that the moment they asked for volunteers I was up, out of my seat, and on to the stage. As Peter grew older this exhibitionist display by his younger brother became too much for him so, out of respect and to save his embarrassment, I remained in my seat. But that meant I went again to the pantomime, this time on my own. Then there was no one to restrain me or stop me having my moment of glory. I was out of my seat and on that stage before anyone could say, 'Oh no he can't.'

14

On one visit to the New Theatre I came away with more than I'd taken with me. Frances Day was topping the bill in variety and I was sitting in the front row of the stalls, missing the orchestra conductor by two. During her act she got the audience to sing 'Gillygillyossenfefercatsenellabogen-by-the-sea'. At the end of it she gave me a prize for singing better than anyone else in the whole theatre. I have to admit that the competition was not that great, as it was first house on a Monday night, but I was thrilled with my prize – a string of sausages. The No 24 bus couldn't get me home soon enough; not only had I come first but I had also won a prize that would ease the strain on the housekeeping money. The reception was not quite as ecstatic as I'd hoped. When Mother took one look at the sausages, she declared that there was no knowing where they had been or who had handled them backstage, and promptly threw them in the dustbin.

In 1985 I was to return to the New Theatre for pantomime, but this time I was in it – and not just for the pantomime song. London Weekend Television was producing the programme *All Star Secrets*, and although, as one newspaper pointed out, I was in no way a 'star' I was asked to be on the panel. Under the chairmanship of Michael Parkinson the panel, consisting of such people as Faith Brown, Roy Kinnear, Ruth Madoc and Kenneth Williams, had to guess which story related to which panellist. At the very end of the show Michael revealed that one of the panel had a secret ambition: it was to play pantomime dame in Cardiff. Unbeknown to me London Weekend Television had arranged with the producer of the Cardiff pantomime, Peter Lea, for me to play one night as dame. The panto starred Stu Francis and Ruth Madoc, and suddenly Stu appeared with a nurse's outfit for me to try on and then and there, on screen, I was given a quick rehearsal for the part.

It was decided that my actual performance should take place on 30 January, my birthday. So as not to upset the smooth running of the show, I worked alongside the real dame, Anna Karen. The only pieces I rehearsed were the ballet scene, the chase through the graveyard and the test under the 'Tree of Truth'. Wardrobe and make-up came up trumps, but before the actual show started, the producer introduced me to the audience, still wearing my suit and dog-collar, and explained what was to happen. The theatre was packed and many of my father's old parishioners and my mother's old Guides, who have been loyal to me over the years, turned out. Some were not sure what would happen, some even wondered whether, this time, I had gone too far. As I left the stage to get into my costume the orchestra played, rather inappropriately, 'When the saints go marching in', and I had also been warned by then that the show was due to end at approximately 10 p.m.

The actors couldn't have been more welcoming and encouraging, but the chorus were a little more cautious about this cuckoo who had suddenly appeared in the nest. They waited in the wings while I made my first entrance and as soon as they had seen that I could cope with the audience they welcomed me into the fold. Once in that fold I felt safe. One of the reasons that I have so enjoyed working with the acting profession is their acceptance, providing you are able to deliver the goods. There may well be some back-biting back stage, but the ultimate aim is to entertain the audience. And that needs teamwork.

When the curtain came down thirty minutes late the orchestra, I am glad to say, was still there, and judging from the level of the applause the audience had obviously enjoyed the evening. As the curtain went up for a final bow a huge birthday cake and champagne arrived on stage, it was Stu Francis' birthday as well as mine. Then the orchestra, possibly to get their own back for the extended evening's work, played the Beatles number 'When I'm sixty-four'.

After the party I went back to the hotel to go to bed. Sleep didn't come easily; running through my head were the tunes, the memories, and the comments of what had been a fantastic evening. For once I had no nagging comments eating away at me; if anyone had disapproved they hadn't said so and I was happy that I had brought together my life as a priest and as an entertainer. Certainly I could not have chosen a better

medium than pantomime, which always has at its centre the triumph of good over evil.

Being an entertainer has always been part of my life. Even as a baby in a pram I used to sit up and smile – an act which always brings a warm response. And from a very early age I realised that I could make people laugh. My speaking voice, even as a child, was fairly deep, so I had only to open my mouth and people were amused with the sound that came out. When Nanny took me out to tea she would often encourage me to make people laugh and so make myself a welcome guest. It's a gift that I still use today and often it has been a life-saver. After the death of my mother, when I was just eighteen, I needed to accept the hospitality of many kind friends and realised that being able to bring laughter into homes is a definite asset. However, I have also learnt over the years that, as with all gifts, there is a dangerous side as well. Humour can at times be offensive and I've always had to guard against causing unnecessary hurt because I have wanted to be funny. It also became a drawback when I realised that I was only being invited to gatherings because I could make people laugh. Like anyone else there are times when the last thing I wanted to be was funny. I trust that my sense of humour has not stopped people taking me seriously and that although every situation, however sad, must have its lighter side, I have tried to be sensitive to the needs of others.

I used humour to see the lighter side of being part of an incomplete family. Whether my father and I would have got on is open to question, but I certainly realised that something was missing in my life. I always looked at other people's fathers with awe and admiration and a certain amount of fear because I was not too sure how to cope with them. I remember saying to my mother once that I wished I had a Daddy, even if he was a burglar. She just laughed. I don't think my mother ever thought of remarriage, but like many widows I don't think she found it easy having to become the bread-winner, the decision-maker and the disciplinarian. House-work was never her greatest love and she was very grateful to Nanny for keeping the home so clean and so welcoming; however she did find her new role very lonely. As children we never went without love, food, clothes or a holiday, but we did go without a father and I think that humour has been one way in which I have compensated for that.

Like any performer I needed an audience and fortunately in the home in Dorchester Avenue there was no shortage. The main supporters were Pat, Pam and Gill. If it was my turn to choose the game it would often be 'Churches'. Here I knew I couldn't go wrong; the ordination of women hadn't been thought of so there was no chance of Pat, Pam or Gill having the starring role. The altar was set up at the top of the steps that led from the french windows in the dining room into the garden. It was the nearest thing I could get to the High Altar in St German's. The congregation were allowed to bring their dolls, and the odd pet as long as it would sit quietly for a few minutes. I was grateful for anything that would swell the congregation. They did not have to enjoy hell-fire sermons, because it was the drama of the liturgy, rather than the strength of the sermon, that originally attracted me to worship. For the communion, Trebor mints served as bread wafers and Vimto was a substitute for wine. On the odd occasion when no one was at home I would add an authentic vestment to the sheet that I used as an alb and the bedspread that I wore as a cope. In my mother's wardrobe there was a box containing my father's stoles. My mother had kept very little of my father's belongings, but as he had hoped that one of his sons would be a doctor and the other a priest, she had kept his stoles. They were regarded as holy things set aside for divine worship, but to me, at that age, they were a piece of authentic glamour which would add just that little bit extra to my performance. Now these stoles are in my own wardrobe and I use them in worship as my father would have wanted them used. Through them and their history I do feel a link with that person whose physical connection was broken from me at such an early age.

2

I PUT AWAY CHILDISH THINGS

The death of my father meant that I was destined to spend most of my early years away from home. A charity called The Clergy Orphan Corporation has two schools: St Margaret's at Bushey, Hertfordshire, for girls and St Edmund's, Canterbury, for boys. And although these schools are open to everyone, they were originally founded to educate the orphaned sons and daughters of the clergy. Now I would question the value of separating a child from his or her home but, at the time, St Edmund's proved to be an absolute godsend. It relieved a great strain on my mother because as well as being educated I was fed, watered and clothed for eight months of the year.

I had been happy enough at Marlborough Road Infants and Junior School, despite the fact that my teacher, Miss Newbury, had to bribe me with a basket of fruit to go for a whole week without crying; for even at an early age they had seen my potential as a performer. They sent me to represent the school to sing around the first civic Christmas tree in Cardiff.

The Easter Eve before I went away to school for the first time, at the age of ten-and-a-half, I was confirmed by the Bishop of Llandaff in St German's. Mummy thought I should be confirmed in my own church and not in a school chapel. As a boat boy and a choirboy I had always felt that I was playing a major part in the communion service, but now I knew I was. To be able to receive the sacrament has always been the great sustainer throughout my life, and although at ten-and-a-half it

is not possible to understand the deeper, theological meaning, communion has always meant to me acceptance, forgiveness and belonging. My confirmation was also the one
significant public occasion which my mother witnessed. By
the time I came to be ordained she had died. But somehow
she knew I would be ordained. I was always thought of as the
one who would follow in his father's footsteps.

On the night before I went away to school, I was a godfather for the first time to Rachel. I now have fifteen god-
children. But the joy and pride of being a godfather was very
much watered down by tears. This was to be my last night at
home for three months, and those tears although they dim-
inished, never really disappeared over the years. I did not like
leaving home; Nanny certainly hated the thought that I was
going away, but Mummy put on a brave face. Peter was more
practical. For a few years we were at school together and to
cheer me up he used to give me a Churchman's No. 1
cigarette. This was meant to generate fifteen minutes' satis-
faction. I am not sure that it achieved that, but it did take my
mind off the fact that it would be another three months before
I was home again. For the next nine years Canterbury was to
be my home for most of the time. I grew to appreciate the
wonderful view the school had of Canterbury Cathedral and I
learnt how to look after myself – a lesson which was to stand
me in very good stead.

Academically I was not a high achiever. Paul Bates and
Robert Atkins always outshone me. But at least my school
reports didn't make too depressing a read. In the Junior
school Mr Littlebury made sure my work was neat and tidy as
he insisted we copied all our work into our 'best books'. What
educationalists would make of that today, I shudder to think.
Sadly the need for tidiness seems to have worn off, you have
only to see my bedroom to realise that.

Mr Cox was my housemaster and it would be hard to think
of anyone better to look after young boys. He was enthusi-
astic, caring and got on extremely well with the matron, Miss
Lester, whom he married thirty or so years later in Papua,
New Guinea. They were a powerful combination whom it was

not wise to cross but whose fairness and generosity I came to appreciate.

Sport played no part at all in my life, though I realise that saying that could be looked on as heresy, but I was, and still am, hopeless at all sport and have very little interest in it. Back pages of newspapers are for ever unread by me. But in a community like an English public school you have to contribute something. My forte was music and drama. Fortunately, at St Edmund's music and drama were seen to be as important as sport – and this was long before they became educational band wagons.

The music was under the direction of Donald Leggett, a very talented musician who expected the highest standards from everyone, including himself. Mr Leggett and I did not see eye to eye. At one practice it actually came to blows. I persistently sang flat, and this was too much for him. He clouted me one across the face taking with him my glasses, which smashed on the floor. For the next five weeks, while my glasses were being mended, I pretended that I could not read or write. My musical abilities may have been limited, but my acting talent was worthy of an Oscar. I even dictated my letters home to my best friend Alan Wackett. He lived locally in Whitstable and he and his parents provided me with a very welcome second home.

If Mr Leggett didn't appreciate my singing voice, he didn't reckon my instrumental ability too highly either. Under the gentle ear of Miss Nancy White, I learnt the cello. But it posed difficulties, both musically and practically. It is not easy to travel from Canterbury to Cardiff carrying a cello and wearing a straw boater. My party piece was called 'Jig' and it was all pizzicato; bows, according to Miss White, were to be brought in at a later stage. When performing this piece for Mr Leggett he failed to appreciate its finer points – he thought the whole piece was part of my tuning up exercises!

Fortunately, at drama I was far more successful; it was, in fact, my lifeline. Under the direction of Philip Hollingworth, a very talented if somewhat volatile man, and Barry Blake, who was equally talented and has remained a good friend ever since, I learnt the joy of theatre. After great success as Toad in *Toad of Toad Hall* I immediately gained admission to the Dramatic Society on entry to the senior school but it was a while before I was back in a starring role. One of my earliest performances was as Roxana in Terence Rattigan's *Adventure Story*. She didn't have a single line to say; all she was expected to do was giggle. This, for me, needed little rehearsal. The standard of drama was high, even if the facilities were a little primitive. The physics labs were the dressing rooms and to gain access backstage you had to cross the playground, climb a ladder and enter through a window; obviously this could only be done between scenes. I remember one December standing on that ladder in the flimsiest of outfits with the snow falling and the distant strains of the Salvation Army Band playing carols. Waiting for an entrance was not a pleasant experience.

As well as straight plays at St Edmund's we did both variety and revue and here I was in my element. Such parts as Lady Macbeth in an American musical version of the play were sheer delight for me, even if both Shakespeare and Marlowe were turning in their respective graves. The sleep-walking scene contained one of the hit numbers; written by Barry Blake and set to music by Chris Peto:

> I cain't sleep,
> Perambulations nocturnal ain't right,
> I'm losing all my beauty,
> Just a has-been cutie,
> A thing that goes bump in the night.
>
> I cain't sleep,
> Believe me boy it's mighty
> Chilly in this nightie,
> I cain't sleep.

My only theatrical failure was as Prospero in Shakespeare's *The Tempest*. It was silly, I should never have tried to go straight. If I was getting laughs I knew where I stood, although this could lead me to going over the top at times. In a very successful production of R. C. Sherriff's *Journey's End* I was playing Totter with Robert Atkins playing Mason. Ours were the only parts to get laughter and on the scenery we kept a score chart of the number of laughs we got. On the first night I received applause on my exit and this was too much for Bob, who was waiting to make his entrance. So on the second night he came in so fast it was impossible for anyone to even move a finger, let alone clap. I was hellbent on revenge, so on the final night I decided not to make an exit at all. I cut several pages of the script, thereby eliminating Bob's appearance in that act altogether. This annoyed Bob, Mr Blake and, I am sure, R. C. Sherriff, but it did mean that my score stayed high as regards laughter.

At the other end of the corridor from the school hall was the school chapel. Because I had arrived at school already confirmed I was able to take a full part in all the worship right from the start. Unlike many of today's public schools the chapel was the real centre of school life and not just an elaborate building to hold christianised assemblies. It was very important that St Edmund's remained true to its Christian foundation in deed as well as word. At that time, the 1950s, there was none of the resistance to compulsory worship that exists today.

To me the chapel was also a link with home. I became chapel monitor and took great delight in looking after the administration of the chapel. Putting out vestments, changing frontals, tidying hymn books, showing visitors to their seats, were all part of my duties. Attendance at the regular weekday celebration of Holy Communion made sure that the sacraments stayed central to my life; it was seen as a normal part of it. I did not see myself as a Holy Joe or part of the God-squad. It was certainly an outlet for my need to be a performer, but it was so much more than that. By being involved with the chapel worship I was keeping alive the memory of my father who, although I never knew, was held in very high regard, and I was pleasing my mother, which for me was very important. I didn't ask deep, searching, theological questions, I just accepted that a person is a spirit as well as a mind and a body and the spiritual side needs as much care as the physical or the mental side. The two chaplains, the Reverend David Mead-Briggs and the Reverend Jack Courtney, were excellent, caring parish priests and served as a good model for me when I was later to become a school chaplain, although the demands for that job had by then changed considerably. Jack Courtney will always hold a special place in my memory.

At the start of this particular term I had travelled up to London a day early to stay with Robert Atkins and his family, and for some unknown reason I had popped into her school to say goodbye to my mother, although we had said goodbye at home. It had been a particularly eventful holiday as for the first time ever we had spent Easter away from home. My mother was a firm believer that Christians should be in their home parish for Easter, but this year we had gone as a family to visit Hawarden, where my father had been a curate and my parents had had their first married home. We made our Easter communion there before travelling on to Prestwich, near Manchester, to stay with my aunt and uncle. Ten days later term was due to begin. After spending the night in London I went back to school the next day, Friday 3 May.

On the following Monday at about 9.15 p.m. I was doing my prep when a monitor came to say that there was someone wanting to speak to me who wanted to talk to the headmaster first. I went along to the headmaster's study to be told that my mother was seriously ill and I was to get home as soon as possible. There had been no warning, she had suffered for years with arthritis and deafness which had made life exhausting for her, but otherwise, to me, she was as strong as they come. She was a big lady; I remember once saying that I was a very lucky boy because I had one mother with the material for two. The headmaster and his wife, Mrs Thoseby, kindly took me to their house and suggested that I should stay the night with them before travelling back to Cardiff in the morning. But they also let Jack Courtney know and he came to visit me immediately. He thought that I should get home as quickly as possible. So there and then he got out his car and drove me to

London. I caught the milk train from Paddington which arrived in Cardiff at about 5.30 a.m. It was the longest journey I've ever made. I couldn't quite realise what was happening, but I read carefully St John's account of the resurrection of Jesus and I kept rereading it. It was as well that I travelled when I did because by midday Mummy had died and my life was turned upside down.

It was now that I realised more than ever the need to be an entertainer. Shortly before my mother died we had gone for a walk. My mother's arthritic hip meant that we took things at a fairly slow pace, so I took the opportunity to tell her that I was beginning to change my mind as regards my future. Instead of ordination I was thinking of going on the stage. Although this must have hurt her, she was extremely sensible. There was none of the 'don't darken my door' routine. She asked me how I intended to set about it and warned me of the difficulties of the theatrical profession, and with that the subject was dropped. With her death the pressure to be ordained increased. Live parents can be fairly effective in persuading their children; dead ones can be even more so.

People couldn't have been kinder. My brother gave me great protection, and when he married Anne the following year, they kindly provided me with a home. Very sadly Nanny had to find a new job although we have always stayed in very close contact. Friends and neighbours also gave me much needed support.

The summer my mother died I had two holidays: the first was with my newly-appointed guardian, the Archdeacon of Chesterfield. He was a complete stranger to me and over the few years that he was responsible for me we didn't manage to achieve a feeling of closeness. He took me on an architectural tour of the north. For the first time I saw the splendours of York, Durham, Ripon and Selby, and with notebook in hand I had to jot down such things of architectural interest as Norman fonts, Broach spires and Clayton and Bell stained-glass windows. The real treat was that for the first time in my life I stayed in smart hotels. The second holiday was with Margaret and Connie. Margaret was a teaching colleague of my mother's and Connie wrote plays for BBC *Children's Hour*. They always went to Stratford and in those days it was possible to see in a fortnight all five Shakespearean plays that were being presented that season. It was a marvellous experience. One play, *Much Ado About Nothing*, I saw three times. First the dress rehearsal, then standing for the first night and then, in the stalls with Margaret and Connie, later in the week. Once again, I was in my element.

Life without a real base was very unsettling. For the first year after my mother's death I was still at school, so that, of course, provided security. But I had to make decisions about the future. I felt that I had to get on with things and now ordination was the sole target on which my sights were set. I got a place at King's College, London, to read theology. After the protection of a boarding school it was quite a shock to find myself travelling from Tulse Hill, in South London, to the Strand every day. But I was determined to make the most of my time at university, despite the fact that in London that was not easy. It was drama that once again became the extra-curricular activity. Both producing and appearing in the college cabaret kept the showbiz side of my soul happy, while the appointment as the college chapel sacristan saw that the spiritual side was not neglected. I have always found well-conducted worship a great strength to me. It can be as spectacular or as simple as you like, but I need to realise that the person taking it has taken the trouble to do this most responsible of activities with care. Badly conducted worship is a huge stumbling block. It makes me very angry. With Sydney Evans as Dean there was no chance of anything connected with worship being slipshod. Even the candles on the altar were set a demanding standard: there was one set to be burnt and one set for show. When the burnt ones reached a certain level, the show ones took their place and a new show set was introduced. Altar linen had to be clean, books tidy and services had to start on time. In no way was God to be offered second best.

At the theological college in Warminster the demands were the same. 'Blessed John of the Lodge', as we called the

Warden, the Reverend John Townrowe, was determined to see that the King's College-educated men were properly trained as regards the ordering of public worship.

Like any student at that time I got various jobs during the vacation. The Post Office supplied employment at Christmas, and during the summer the work ranged from dealing with dead pensioners' records to window dressing at Barkers in Kensington. Well, to be honest, window dressing was only a very small part of the job. I was really an assistant in the bedding department. In the main I was kept a good distance from the customers. Carting beds to and from the fourth floor was my main responsibility and in those days the beds travelled in the same lifts as the cooked meats, so either I put my mattresses on the cooked chickens or the cooked chickens had a very comfortable ride on my mattresses. The one spell of window dressing I was allowed was of a tiny corner window. All I had to do was place a set of bunk-beds in the window at a certain angle. I made a meal of it, so much so that at the end it turned out to be a cabaret performance: I had attracted quite an audience. One summer there was no chance of getting a vac job. I had been appointed leader of the King's College Mission to the hop-pickers. This took place in September, when the East Enders packed up everything, including the kitchen sink, and headed for the hop fields of Kent. Mechanisation was just starting, but still many East Enders made this annual pilgrimage their summer holiday. They converted their huts into palaces. Grandma and the budgie were not forgotten, nor were the great cockney songs which rang out in the pub each night.

As a missioner you visited the people as they were picking, but you had to make sure you didn't slow down the picking rate. In fact you were expected to contribute to it. It also meant that you had to keep on the move, for to show one family more favour than another could cause a great loss in possible converts. The part of the mission which was most appreciated was the work with the children; not necessarily by the children, but certainly by their parents. Each evening we would run a sort of Sunday School where we presented the

Bible stories as drama while the parents prepared the evening meal. In the Middle Ages the people of York, Coventry, Wakefield and Lincoln had all been taught the Bible by means of drama. The Miracle Plays which belong to those cities were the ways in which they learnt not just the Bible itself but also a theological interpretation of a deeper meaning of some of the stories. And so we were only repeating a tried and tested method with the children of 1960 as we tried to interest them in the person of Jesus. The experience was demanding. Sharp cockney minds didn't let you get away with anything and this was quite unnerving for those of us who, after several years of theological study, thought that we'd got the whole faith thing buttoned up. The day ended in a slightly more relaxed mood as we joined the parents in the pub before returning to our huts for the late-night service of compline and bed.

The strain of the mission proved too much for me physically. As a very young child, it was discovered that I had a slight heart murmur, and now and again, when the pressure is great, it has suggested that I take life a little easier. The heart started complaining again and I spent quite a bit of the time trying to direct things from my bed in the local vicarage. Physical comforts were few, but the one we did appreciate was the weekly bath at the home of the local squire, Viscount Falmouth. I was to be reminded of that touch of luxury about fifteen years later. I was teaching St Mark's gospel to fourteen year olds at Eton College and when the lesson ended one of the boys came to me and said, 'Sir, didn't you used to come to our home for a bath once?' It was the son and heir to the title. My bath must have become part of the historical records of the Falmouth family.

Academic success had, on the whole, eluded me – and still does – but during my time at King's I won two prizes: both were theological, both also needed an understanding of drama. The first was the liturgy prize; the development and conduct of worship has always been of interest to me. The second was the sermon prize: it was on the text 'Behold the man'. Sermon preparation was part of our training at Warminster. The greatest ordeal of all was sermon class. In turn each of us had to prepare and declare a sermon at the end of which, unlike Church of England congregations who either say nothing or just say, 'Thank you, Vicar', it was torn to pieces by our colleagues. Obviously this was done in charity, although it did not always seem too evident at the time. Other disciplines like baptising a baby or visiting the sick seemed much easier things to practise, but it wasn't just our fellow students who suffered.

Local parishes kindly allowed us to practise worship and preaching on live congregations. The people of the parish of Westbury and Westbury Leigh were particularly long-suffering. Not only did they have to suffer sermons but also the way we read the lesson, said the prayers and sang the service. As regards singing, my broken voice was a little more reliable than my treble voice, but the same could not be said of the colleague who accompanied me each week to Westbury. He had a voice that would shatter glass, stained glass at that. In the middle of one service the organist sent frantic signals to try and stop him singing, but to no avail. He is now the Archdeacon of Rochdale – Gracie Fields must be wondering what has happened to her home town!

Although David may have had difficulties with his singing voice, there was no reason for any of us to be inaudible when speaking or reading. This was thanks to our elocution teacher Audrey Bullard, known affectionately as Auntie. She had no objection whatsoever to accents, but she did object if you muttered. Proper breathing was to be the cure for most, if not all, speaking problems. It could also cure that terrible disease 'Parsonic voice'. To do the breathing exercises you first had to find your diaphragm. That was not always easy, and for one student it proved impossible. So she called him out in front of the class so that he could put his hands on her diaphragm and thus experience what proper breathing was all about. Auntie began to breathe deeply and asked the student what he could feel. 'Corsets, ma'am' was his reply. 'Go to the Dean,' she commanded in a voice that had its own in-built quadrophonic sound. I shall always be grateful to Auntie, for as well as teaching us to speak 'proper' she also helped us to prepare short talks, make votes of thanks and introduce speakers, all of which has stood me in good stead throughout my ministry. Warminster was also a time when we tried to put in the foundations of a proper spiritual life. Away from the distractions of London it was ideal to look at priorities. As a future priest, prayer was to be one of them. I have never found private prayer easy. With the sort of mind I have, which constantly flits from one thing to another, the command to 'Be still and know that I am God' has always been a difficult one to obey. 'Arrow' prayers I can shoot up thick and fast, both for others and myself, because they are immediate and very much related to the present moment, but I have really to discipline myself to set aside a time to remember the special presence of God. I have been fortunate in the senior priests that I have had as spiritual directors. A former Dean of Westminster, whom I first met at the Mermaid Theatre watching the Wakefield Mystery Plays, kept a very good eye on my spiritual growth during those early years. And Canon

Derek Allen helps me to make sure these days that I remember my vocation as a priest, even though I spend more time in front of microphones and cameras than I do in church.

One thought which dominated all my spiritual as well as my secular thoughts during my time at Warminster was, where should I serve my title? Which parish was to have the ordeal of putting me through my paces and turning me into a priest who knew his job and got on with it? It was to be the very famous parish of St Mary's Portsea, in Portsmouth. Its vicars and curates often became archbishops, bishops, deans and archdeacons. I am not sure that they ever envisioned producing someone who was destined to appear on television game shows.

3

FISHERS OF MEN

The hunt for a parish that would have me had not been easy. I was sent first of all to a parish in London; it was a working-class parish with a strong streak of so-called 'top people' living in it. With fear in my heart I arrived at the vicarage at the appointed time on a Saturday afternoon. I was very much attracted to the parish but I soon began to have my doubts. One of the questions I was asked was whether my teeth were my own. I could not quite see what bearing that had on my possible appointment as a curate. To the question whether I would be afraid of eating with the rich, I replied that I could always watch and then follow suit, a policy that I later had to put into practice many times during my stay at Eton.

The vicar was only prepared to have curates who were public school boys, and when I questioned him on this he replied, 'Well, you see, Roger, if there was any housekeeping money over at the end of the month public school boys would know to buy another bottle of sherry, rather than a more expensive lavatory paper.' This I couldn't take and, to be fair to the vicar, he did later apologise for making the remark, but it was one of those remarks that just stuck in your mind. I always dread it when I make a remark which is meant to be funny but somehow to the other person's ear it just isn't, and it's very difficult to take back the things you say.

I wasn't too surprised when I received a letter telling me that I was not being offered a curacy at that parish. The reason given was that the vicar didn't feel my health would be able to cope with all the stairs in the tenement flats.

The next parish I was due to visit was a complete non-starter. Before he had even seen me, the vicar had decided that he did not need a curate. Come to think of it, some curates are more bother than they are worth, so he probably made a wise decision.

However, the Reverend Canon F. S. Temple, at St Mary's Portsea, Portsmouth, was prepared to see me. Once again I went to stay for the weekend and this visit was far less of an ordeal. I was introduced to some of the eleven other curates and warned that three of the churches in the parish would be closing six months before I arrived. This was something of a comfort as it meant that my arrival could in no way be blamed for the closures. By the end of the weekend I was offered the job and I was very thrilled, but the excitement was somewhat dampened when my guardian received the news. He wondered why I was going to so vast and featureless a church, which set such moderate standards.

The whole business of choosing a parish, or being ordained at all, is very difficult. I have never received a blinding-light conversion like St Paul; few, I believe, are so privileged to receive such things. I have not heard voices telling me what to do either; it just seemed that this was what I was meant to do. Already I had to leave it to others to decide whether I was suitable or not, and I think there are some people who are still undecided! All I did know was that by being ordained I would have delighted my parents and I know that I delighted many of their friends. Whether that's a good enough reason, I have to leave God to be my judge.

I am not quite sure what you are meant to look for when you are seeking your first curacy. You are obviously not meant to put creature comforts high on the list, but you do have to go where you feel God can use you. Also, as a curate, you have to realise that the parish is going to be more use to you than you to the parish. In those first three years you have a lot to learn and it is only really in the third year that you are any use to God, man or beast.

There had been a slight worry that in choosing Portsmouth I was choosing something a little too comfortable. During my time at King's I had each week gone down to the Franciscans in Cable Street, in London's East End, to teach English to

people of West Indian origin. It had been quite an ordeal and
certainly an eye-opener. As I made my way down Leman
Street I would run from lamp-post to lamp-post; 'see and
be seen' is my motto – although I would have been happier
if I had not seen two women having a bottle fight one
evening.

The Franciscan House had a simplicity which I am sure
would have pleased St Francis. The friar, Father Neville, who
lived there was a very humble man who lived, to the full, the
humble lifestyle that was demanded of him. However, he did
keep a pot of vegetable stew on the stove, and the level never
seemed to go down, although it provided sustenance for all
who called.

One of the families I taught was the Shabi family. We
battled away together to conquer this language which seems
to break every rule in the book and through our ordeal we
became friends, so much so that when the family were to be
baptised I was asked to be Desmond's godfather. They were a
fascinating family to visit because they lived at the top of a
small tenement house. They shared their landing with one
other family, the Shalankis. Mrs Shalanki had an unusual
profession – she was a fire-eater. Regularly she would appear
on the landing in her black bra and panties, swallowing huge
sheets of flame in the same way that you or I might swallow an
aspirin. How the house never caught fire I shall never know.
Visiting the East End once a week was one thing, but I doubt
that I would have had the stamina to go there for my first
curacy.

Three days before I was made deacon in Portsmouth
Cathedral, I went on a retreat along with the others who were
due to be ordained. It's not easy for me to keep quiet at the
best of times and it certainly wasn't easy three days before I
was about to make the biggest commitment that I had ever
made. Fortunately things happened to relieve the tension. On
the night before I was ordained I went to the chapel at the
retreat house for the evening service of compline. Kneeling
next to me was Malcolm Johnson, who was due to serve in the
next-door parish of St Mark's. I found the place in my prayer

...stopping for a bite of lunch?

book and put it in front of me waiting for the service to begin.
Suddenly Malcolm removed the book and replaced it with
another prayer book open at the service for the consecration
of bishops. It was a while before I could get my thoughts back
to things celestial.

The morning of the ordination dawned. I think the biggest
problem that confronted me was how to get my dog-collar on.
It was in the days when linen collars were worn for important
occasions; the plastic ones that you just wipe in the morning
when you clean your teeth were kept as everyday collars and
the thought of cutting a piece out of the Fairy Liquid bottle
and sticking it under my collar had never entered my head –
then. However, the struggle was won, the collar was on, and

there I stood in a brand new cassock, looking every inch the new curate – either that or an extra in one of Derek Nimmo's churchy comedies.

The service in Portsmouth Cathedral was quiet and ordered. All those to be ordained were herded into the mayor's pew and then the door was shut. There was no chance of escaping now. The bishop of the diocese was ill, so his part was taken by an understudy. The service seemed to go on and on and there was certainly no chance of it being good theatre. Portsmouth Cathedral is a hotch-potch of a building and everyone seems to have had a go at adding a little bit to it, so it was well nigh impossible to get a clear view of everything that was going on.

The sermon, I remember, was by a Franciscan and it talked of us as having been branded as cattle are branded; it is a mark of a good sermon that it still lives with me twenty-five years later.

After the service I gathered with my friends and family for a celebratory lunch at which the main topic of conversation seemed to be, 'Oh, doesn't he look like his father?' But as the afternoon drew on my supporters had to make their way home and I got ready to appear in the parish for the first time as the new curate.

I had only a small part to play at evensong – I had to read a lesson and swear loyalty and obedience. Fortunately the lesson, which was from the Old Testament, contained none of those totally unpronounceable names. I lost my fear for those names when I was given a little hint by a fellow ordinand. 'I never bother with them,' he said. 'If it's a place-name then I say he went to the south or the north and if it's a person I change their name to Joseph, David or Benjamin, and then I have no trouble at all.' I am not quite sure what a biblical scholar would make of it, but it certainly made life a lot easier for me.

The biggest problem of that first night in the parish was remembering parishioners' names. I met a great sea of faces and was introduced to countless people and they were all kind enough to say that they didn't expect me to remember their names, but somehow I had a feeling that life would be a lot easier if I did remember them.

One name I learnt straight away and have never forgotten was Pro Luckham. She was the sacristan of St Mary's and I think she had been training curates since Augustine first landed on these shores. She was marvellous and she was a great disciplinarian. Woe betide you if you tried to go into church looking scruffy. She would never tell you off in front of the choir. She would ask you quietly, but firmly, to step back into the vestry and then she would sort you out. No actor could have had a finer dresser. She also told you what she thought of your sermons, and it wasn't just a quick comment. Pro gave a detailed criticism of what she saw as both the contents of your sermon and its delivery. Every curate who was trained at St Mary's while Pro was still alive has a lot to thank her for. When I left the parish she had a beautiful cope made for me with enough material left over to make a mitre should the call of the purple come my way. Where that piece of material has got to now I have no idea – still, somehow I doubt that I shall need it!

The rules of the clergy house were fairly strict. It didn't pay to oversleep in the morning; to arrive at breakfast having missed matins and communion was not acceptable. However, it did serve as quite a good rehearsal for the final judgment – although come to think of it the final judgment may be a little bit easier.

In times of trouble you could always turn to Mr and Mrs A – the housekeepers. Mrs A's cooking was first class; nothing fancy, but everything healthy. She was determined that none of her curates would be wilting violets.

Being the junior curate meant that you had to be good with children, and so I was soon made responsible for the Sunday School. This followed the 11.15 family service, which lasted half an hour, and those thirty minutes were fun-packed, to say the least. The vicar believed that if we were to hold the attention of the children we had to use visual aids in our sermon, and he insisted that they were called visual aids, not gimmicks. I agreed with him entirely, as did my fellow curate,

Alun Glyn-Jones. The only trouble was finding the visual aid. At one time it got to the stage where you found the visual aid first and then found a point to make out of it. One thing was certain, you didn't let on what you had, for fear that Alun or the vicar would swipe it before you had a chance to use it!

I was unlucky because I had to take the Whit Sunday service two years running. It is not easy to find a visual aid for the Holy Spirit. The first year Esso came to my rescue. It was at the time when they were running the advertising campaign which had as a slogan, 'Put a Tiger in Your Tank' and many people were driving round with a little tiger's tail hanging from their petrol cap. So, under the cover of darkness, I borrowed the big display tiger from the local garage and managed to hide it in the choir stalls until the appropriate moment. It seemed to go down well, after all the Holy Spirit is an unseen force rather like the unseen tiger which was meant to be the power behind your car.

The following year it was very much harder to think of something new. Suddenly I thought it would be good to show the children the various symbols which represent the Holy Spirit: fire was easy, it was just a matter of lighting a candle; wind posed few problems because in those days people still had bellows; but what about the dove? The thought of a dove, or even a pigeon, fluttering around the church fairly terrified me because I am not too good with our feathered friends. So I ended up with a budgie in a cage, but the only trouble was that the little bird would not keep quiet, so there was a merry chirping throughout the service.

The very first family service I took, I came down the aisle in a boiler suit, pushing a barrow-load of bricks. Now I can't remember whether that was to illustrate the stone which the builders rejected or building your house upon rock – whichever one it was, it seemed to be enjoyed.

For the Feast of the Ascension I managed to persuade the vicar to go up the church tower and from a spy-hole he was able to do a double-act with me on the chancel step. This, I hasten to add was to show how *not* to think about the

Ascension, but when you come to think of it, artists through-out the ages have found the Ascension difficult to represent: a couple of feet sticking out of a cloud is open to as much misinterpretation as a vicar up a church tower.

Even the sombre season of Lent allowed for a little drama. On Wednesday afternoons, after school, I ran a Lent course for children. It was always based on such gripping titles as 'Johnny and the Seven Dreadful Giants', but even with a title like that I thought it was essential to add that little bit extra. How I got hold of it I have no idea, but I did manage to get a Dalek from the BBC television series *Dr Who*. At playtime I nipped round all the local schools to spread the good news that if they came to church they would see a Dalek. I suppose it was not quite the same as using a mustard seed, a fig tree or a lost sheep – but it wasn't far off. The church was packed and like all theatrical presentations the star was kept to the end. While the children were all quietly kneeling, under the cover of the blessing, the Dalek was wheeled into the back of the church. The service ended, the children spotted their star and tore, at breakneck speed, to see it. Previous vicars like Archbishop Lang and Archbishop Garbett must have been turning in their graves, but for the children it was an experi-ence which they remembered for a long time. Whether they also remembered the spiritual message of the service is another matter, but then that's always a danger of visual aids.

There was another hazard with the family service – milk bottle tops. As well as the ordinary collection we also col-lected silver paper in aid of the Guide Dogs for the Blind, and this collection consisted mainly of milk bottle tops which, despite regular pleas, came unwashed. As I bent over the tea-chest which was the receptacle in which they were put, I found the children jamming the odd top down my surplice or into my cassock pocket, and you need more than Aramis to conquer this smell. How the Cox family coped I shall never know. It was their act of Christian service to sort out all this paper and to clean these tops. I can only think that they invested a great deal of money in air-fresheners.

My experience with the children in the hop fields stood me

in good stead with the Sunday School. I had a marvellous team of teachers who couldn't have been more dedicated. I am not quite sure how I would have survived without Sheila, Jean and John, as well as people like Miss Ferbrache, who had been teaching in Sunday School since Adam was a child. She was of the old school and the children adored her.

The regular commitment week by week is very demanding but it has its rewards. One reward it certainly didn't have was helping with the annual outing. What possessed us to take two hundred children on the Solent for a day I shall never know, but the Lord was obviously on our side and not once did we return with any children missing or in need of expert medical attention.

If children were missing from Sunday School for a while it was my job to find out why the little lambs had strayed. Some of the excuses were interesting, to say the least. But I think I got the biggest surprise when I knocked on one door: it was opened very slightly, 'Yes, what do you want?' shouted the lady on the other side. 'I am the curate from St Mary's,' I replied. 'I've come to see why Tracy hasn't been to Sunday School for the last couple of weeks.' 'Oh, thank God for that,' came the reply. 'Come in, I thought you were the Cruelty man.'

On another such visit things didn't go quite so well. When I called at the house I was welcomed in, almost with open arms. Stupidly I forgot one of the rules I had been given about visiting: never sit on a settee. We soon got off the subject of why the daughter had been missing from Sunday School and on to the more detailed problems of the mother herself. As the problems started to pour out thick and fast the mother gradually moved round the room, from seat to seat, until she was sitting next to me on the settee. By this time the arms had been opened as she lunged forward to hug me. I moved sharply to a single chair to one side. Even this action was not enough to cool the amorous advances of this particular lady. She approached again. I leapt to my feet and made a bee-line for the front door, and shot out into the street. I don't think I have ever pedalled so fast on my bicycle!

Visiting is not the simple exercise it's made out to be and I am very sorry that these days, in some cases at least, very little visiting is done. There is a definite truth in the old slogan that a home-going priest makes a church-going parish. Some visiting can be very restful.

I remember one old dear whom I called to see who could not have made me more welcome. Naturally she showed me into the front room. This room was only used for such things as entertaining the clergy and laying out the corpse – although I do realise that in some circumstances it is not easy to tell the difference.

I was immediately offered a cup of tea (an offer you can never refuse for fear of offending people). Apparently my father, who could not drink strong tea, had a way of dealing with this. While the person wasn't looking he poured his cup of tea over the plants. History doesn't record whether Splott suffered a high degree of plant deaths.

Having been offered the tea, the kettle was put on a low gas. Hoping that the proverb, 'a watched pot never boils' would come true, this then, of course, cut down the talking time. My hostess returned with the tea and some of her home-made cakes. She started to tell me her life history. Concentration wasn't easy as I couldn't see her face for the aspidistras and potted palms. She had turned this front room into something that resembled a hot house in Kew Gardens. Gradually, sleep took over. The humid atmosphere, plus the lady's gentle voice, got the better of me. Soon my eyes closed and my mind went into neutral. It was two hours before I came to, and when I did I was covered in confusion. By this time my hostess had kindly left me and had gone about her rather more important chores. I called out and began a long sequence of apologies, but she stopped me in mid-flow saying that she took it as a compliment that I was able to be so relaxed in her home. Isn't it great when people think positively?

Visits before funerals were essential but sometimes very harrowing. I am sure that I was helped by my own personal experience; I trust that I never tried to comfort people with false hopes. However I did think that it was vital that I tried to get across the knowledge that death was not the end. Visiting the families of children who had died was the most difficult because not only was there tremendous grief but there was also anger. I shall never forget two children whose funerals I took. The first was in Portsmouth. When I visited the family I found that they had the child still at home in an open coffin surrounded by his toys. All I could do was weep with them and then try and help them to see beyond the tiny corpse in the white coffin to a hope in the future both for him and for them. It certainly was no good saying, 'Everything will be all right' or 'You'll get over it'; it was important to accept the reality of what those parents were feeling there and then.

The second was a young child called Alexander who lived in Dorney. I'd gone to bed at about 10 p.m. that Easter Day. It had been an exhausting day because there had been all the special services to be planned and taken, and on top of that I'd had to supervise an Easter egg race down the church lane, as well as officiate at a service on a roundabout which signalled the start of the village fair. Mind you I'm not complaining, because it did enable me to have a ride on the dodgems with the current Miss World.

I was just dozing off to sleep when the telephone rang. It was two parishioners who were also great friends of mine phoning to tell me that their young son Alexander was dying of leukaemia. They were calling from Great Ormond Street Hospital. Within seconds I was out of bed, dressed, in the car, and on my way to London. When I arrived the child was asleep, so the parents and I went to a nearby late-night cafe. Together we prepared for the future; it wasn't easy, but it did help ease a little of the strain that occurred when Alexander died. His funeral service was quite stunning. The little church was packed and the atmosphere was one of thanksgiving, despite the shortness of his life on this earth. No life is ever wasted and death is certainly not a punishment.

However, I am glad to say that there is a lighter side to funerals. There was one widow and son I visited in Portsmouth the day after the husband died. They were not church people, so they were a little apprehensive about a call from the curate. They made me welcome and after hearing how the husband died, the son soon started teaching me cockney rhyming slang. Although they had lived in Portsmouth for some time, they had not forgotten their roots. The visit became really good fun, but after about an hour I thought I had better explain the service to them and take my leave. As I got up to go the widow thumped the table and said, 'That's the best laugh I've had since hubby died.' As he had only died the previous day, I thought, 'Oh Roger, you've got it wrong again,' but as I cycled back to the clergy house I thought that laughter had been a great healer in my life so why shouldn't God use it to heal other people.

I've always found undertakers the most caring of people. They do have a very real ministry, and they also have a great sense of theatre. Alf Smith on the St Helier estate where I served my second curacy was in the best tradition of Sir Donald Wolfit and the bereaved really appreciated it. There was no question about his sincerity, it was just that he, like all the undertakers I have worked with, realised that dignity is an essential part of the service. But even undertakers have got to see the lighter side of life.

Travelling back in the empty hearse from Porchester crematorium, the driver had suddenly to jam on the brakes to

'Room for one inside!'

avoid hitting an elderly lady who had walked off the pavement and straight into the path of his oncoming hearse. The driver honked the horn, the lady looked up terrified. 'If you do that once more,' you'll be in here,' joked the driver. I thought the old dear was going to have a heart attack there and then, but I should have realised that undertakers do not tout for trade.

I had one firm rule with undertakers: while the coffin and the mourners were still with us there should be no idle chatter. I knew that if they started to tell me something and I found it funny I wouldn't have been able to control my giggles and this, I thought, would have given an extremely wrong impression to the bereaved, as well as adding needlessly to their suffering.

I used to loathe taking contract funerals, or what have been at one time called paupers' funerals. I don't believe that anyone should pass away unmourned, so I either produced some parishioners to come to the service or asked the undertakers themselves to join me. They were not always too keen to do this, but in the end they gave in. I would also try to round up a few flowers. I can understand why people don't want lots of money spent on flowers, although I do think that a few can take the edge off the sombreness of the occasion, but I certainly can't understand why people say 'no letters'. They may bring tears at the time, but often they are wonderful things to treasure and give you a chance to realise that the one you loved was loved by others.

The people of Portsmouth were keen to use the local paper, the *Portsmouth Evening News*, to express their thanks to those who helped them through their bereavement. The paper arrived at the clergy house at about 5 p.m. and there was fierce competition as to who got his hands on the paper first. Instead of turning to the sports page, we turned to the 'thanks for sympathy' column and were always quite thrilled when we were named. This occurred fairly frequently because as a parish we did about thirty-five funerals a week and I believe that it was slightly ironic that when I moved out of that clergy house a firm of undertakers moved in.

4

THE HARVEST IS READY

It wasn't always a matter of death, there was quite a lot of life, and new life at that. St Mary's was never short of baptisms and I had a sneaking feeling that baptisms went up when certain ships were in port. There were some defence cuts I approved of entirely! Preparation classes for baptism always took place the previous week. Here, again, you were sometimes dealing with people whose link with the church was fairly tenuous. They were easy to detect as they would generally say that they would like to have their baby 'done'. I was never quite sure what they wanted done to them.

The idea of someone having a private baptism was out of the question. We may not have been doing thirty-five baptisms a week but the numbers were always high. Possibly we were not strict enough as to whom we baptised, but the one rule was that you had to live in the parish and I do believe that you can never actually refuse to baptise a child. And what is more, the occasion does give such a wonderful opportunity for evangelism and pastoral care. Nor can you expect people to accept that after centuries of baptising children willy-nilly the church should suddenly bring in tougher rules.

Mind you, I could have done with some tougher rules one Whit Sunday. Being a festival it had been a busy morning and then at 3 p.m. I was faced with baptising nineteen babies. Here it was essential to have a sense of theatre. I got a font, a large jug of water, and I'd taken a couple of aspirin. I'd also taken the special precaution of wearing a drip-dry surplice as on these occasions there was no knowing where the water would come from!

All was going extremely well until I reached babe number

fourteen who, instead of being a beautiful child nestling sweetly in its mother's arms, was a bouncing four year old. Well I wasn't prepared to hold a four year old for any length of time, so I put a chair by the side of the font. The grandmother, who was also the godmother, brought the child to the font. To the question 'Name this child,' she replied 'Norman.' So in a very sweet and fatherly way I turned to Norman, 'Come on Norman, jump up on this chair,' to which he replied, 'Shan't.' Act quickly, I thought. I picked Norman up and stood him on the chair. I then suggested that he might like to show some co-operation by bending his head over the front. But Norman was far more quick-witted than I was. He put his hands up over his face so that it was impossible to get any water near or by him without drowning both him and his clothes.

Now I realised that I musn't get angry with this child who was reluctant to recognise the fact that he was a child of God. So I kept my smile the whole time, otherwise people would say 'What a nasty vicar, no wonder no one comes to church.' But all forms of persuasion failed and soon the mother appeared at the font as re-enforcement. You could see what was going through her mind: there were the sandwiches under a damp cloth, the kettle on a low gas, the cake had been made, and she was going to have Norman 'done' if it killed her. Despite her threats Norman still held out. It was time to bring out the big guns. In the firmest of voices she turned to Norman and said, 'I'll get your father to you.' I looked up and there, coming down the aisle at great speed, was a huge hulk of a man who was obviously going to deal Norman a swift blow. Well I wasn't wanting a punch-up on a Whit Sunday after- noon, so I said in what was to become my best TV compère's voice, 'Can you come back next week?' Norman was removed from the font, peace was restored, and the service of Holy Baptism continued. Somehow, I had not been prepared at theological college for Norman, and I also wondered if Nor- man would be able to sort out in his own mind the difference between the father who was going to give him a quick clip around the ear and the Father to whom he was about to pray, who is loving, kind, the supplier of his daily bread, and someone who could protect him from temptation. I often wonder what happened to Norman.

Weddings are a far more frequent hazard. For one thing there's the bride's father and you can never be sure what he will get up to. Many fathers, with justifiable pride, feel that it's their day also and they are not going to miss the opportunity, especially if they are footing the bill. There have been times when I have had to keep them away from any naked light, so great has been the alcohol content of their breath. A breath test for brides' fathers would be quite a good thing, although I do realise that many of them are tremendously nervous.

Again, Portsmouth seemed to produce a great number of marriages. The most we ever did on a single Saturday was sixteen. We, as curates, had a union rule which said that we never did more than five on the trot. After five you had no idea who was coming down the aisle.

The whole thing was meticulously organised. Weddings took place every half hour. The bride came in through the north porch, went out by the great west doors, and had photographs taken by the south door. It worked perfectly, providing no one was late. It only needed one bride to be late and suddenly you had delays that even British Rail would be jealous of, or a tail-back almost as far as Southsea Pier.

Every evening one of us would sit in the vestry with the parish clerk, Will Robinson or Mrs Whurr, and take down the details. Some of the requests were quite interesting. In my second parish, the St Helier Estate in South London, a young couple came in one day and asked to get married so I took down all the relevant details. The bride asked if it was possible to have any hymns. 'Yes, of course you can,' I replied, 'but it will be £5 extra.' (Well, it's no use being so full of heavenly thoughts that you are no earthly use, and the choir had to be paid.) I produced the regular menu: 'Lead us Heavenly Father lead us', 'Love divine', 'The Lord's my Shepherd'. This was essential because some of the people only knew a few Christmas carols, the odd morning hymn from school assembly and 'Abide with Me' from the cup final. I resisted suggesting 'Fight the Good Fight' or 'Through the Night of Doubt and Sorrow'. When the bride looked at the list she said, 'Vicar, the hymn we want isn't on here.' 'Well, as long as it's in the hymn book', came the reply, 'you can certainly have it, what is it?' 'Climb every mountain.' I took a gulp and wondered what was the best way to cope with that. 'I'm terribly sorry, but we don't have that one, but we have got "Hills of the North Rejoice".' 'That'll do nicely,' she replied.

Many of the couples I married were not used to appearing as stars in public. Although they were given preparation classes beforehand and a rehearsal the previous Saturday, when the actual day came the nerves often got the better of them. I did assure them that I was the only person who could see their faces and could whisper everything to them so they couldn't possibly go wrong, but this didn't overcome the worry of making a mistake. For me the biggest nightmare was the bride's veil. There was always the fear that it would either get caught in the grating or the bridegroom would step on it, or a fight would break out between the bridesmaids and the pages and it would be torn apart. I have never been a great believer in children taking on these roles. They may look sweet but, my word, they can detract from the bride and groom. Also fear and panic can seize them, with the result that the bride's mother is not the only one in tears.

But a new hazard dawned with one of the royal weddings. (I think it was Princess Anne's). They always set the style for the weddings that come soon after the event. The dresses may not always cost as much as the royal equivalent but as a lookalike it often wasn't a bad effort. However this particular royal had decided to have her hair built up, a tiara placed in the middle of it, and the veil coming from it. With all the care she gets this presented no problems, but for those of us living in slightly humbler circumstances it added an unexpected hazard. I am a firm believer that wedding vows should not be taken behind veils, so during the first hymn or when the bride arrives at the chancel step, I put the bride's veil back. This worked wonders until the day that the bride decided that her veil and hair-do should resemble the royal's. As I went to put back the veil the whole superstructure came apart in my hands. I expected tears but instead I got a smile and in the remaining four verses of the hymn I struggled valiantly to re-erect the edifice.

The people of Portsmouth and those on the St Helier estate did not normally send formal invitations to the person who was officiating at their wedding. Often, during the last hymn at St Helier, after I'd reminded the newly-married couple of what they had to do at the end of the service, the groom would say to me, 'Doing anything tonight, vicar?' 'Putting the finishing touches to my sermon,' I would generally reply. 'Well then, you can spare a few minutes to pop into the GLC club/The Rose/Community Centre/St Helier Arms for a quick drink.' By the end of the afternoon I had my evening planned. I had to go easy on the drink, but I always made sure I had a dance with the bride before leaving. It was great being able to share in their celebrations on their terms rather than just seeing them in church.

When I started doing 'up-market' weddings life became a lot more difficult. Whereas the people of Portsea and St Helier were prepared to accept my advice, knowing that I would do the best that I possibly could for them, other people had their own ideas of what they wanted and sometimes it was almost necessary to bring in ACAS to make sure that everything was done properly.

I thoroughly enjoy taking weddings. It's glorious sharing so intimately on such an important day. And I have to admit that it still hurts me when I hear that a marriage I have performed has broken up, because I always feel that in some way I have let the couple down.

Visiting is, I believe, an important part of parish life. Visiting the families of Sunday School children can be hazardous, but visiting the elderly has always been a great joy. Some of them may be a bit crotchety, but in the main they are very appreciative of the time you spend with them. From many of the elderly I have drawn great spiritual strength. Their courage, faith, and sense of humour has always been a great encouragement to me. Mrs Denmead, whom I visited once a month with Holy Communion, always strengthened me. I visited her on the first Thursday every month and by the side of her chair she had a little prayer box which was part of her daily routine. I shall never be able to be grateful enough to Doris Probert who has coped with my ups and downs, and I know remembers me constantly in her prayers. She started to go blind during my time on the St Helier estate and each week in Lent I would go to her, read her my Lenten address, and have tea. Since then she has remained a very firm friend.

Most Friday mornings in Portsmouth I would take communion to an old people's home. The wards I visited were on the rather unfortunately named 'Chronic Block'. Sometimes, some of the ladies would want to give their communion to their dolls, and with one particular lady I had a real struggle. I put the communion bread straight into her mouth and she immediately took it out again. I popped it back, she removed it yet again saying, 'I'll keep it till you've gone.' 'No you won't,' I said, and ate it myself. In no way was this old dear being irreverent, but sometimes a confused mind can make something which they obviously treasure seem difficult.

The one thing I wasn't trained for at theological college was the collecting, sorting and pricing of jumble. Under the eagle eye of Mrs Phillips, who was Portsea's jumble queen, I soon learnt. After I had been in the parish a few months, I passed my driving test and bought an Austin mini-van. Nothing could have been better for jumble, but even I was not prepared for one occasion. The husband had died and I had taken the funeral and I called to visit the widow about a week later to see how she was getting on. There was just one thing that was troubling her; how could she get rid of her husband's clothes? "Simple," said I, "you give them to me and I'll take them to the next jumble." She was very grateful and we quickly loaded the van. Just as I was about to leave she asked if I would like the budgie as well. I tried to persuade her to keep it as it would be company for her, but she said she couldn't as it reminded her too much of her husband. I'd have tried even harder to persuade her if I'd realised that although she was keen to get rid of the budgie, she didn't want to part with the

cage. So I had to drive around the parish with the bird flying around the van until I could find a family who were willing to give it a good home.

My dramatic talents were used at the Harvest Supper entertainment. Alun Glyn-Jones usually wrote the excellent scripts and he and I were expected to play the fool to amuse the parishioners. The entertainment was always suitable for the whole family and we had to be careful that we did not take off anybody too severely. But the one thing I did realise was that through harmless mucking about you could get closer to people. Very few thought it was lowering the tone of the clergy, but those few who did would only want to keep their clergy locked up in church.

It was during my time at Portsmouth that I was sent on my first television training course. It was at the Church's Television Centre at Bushey, an institution that had behind it the inspiration and the money of that good Methodist, Lord Rank.

Although it had been made very plain to me that this was only a training course, the moment I sat in front of a camera I thought I was well on my way to stardom. The old business of using my personality and being a priest is a difficult one to handle. Some people believe that it goes completely against my calling, but I am afraid that my calling was not as simple as that. In realising that I have a responsibility to show people Jesus, I am constantly aware of John the Baptist's words that, 'He must increase and I must decrease.' But I also believe that Jesus was prepared to use his personality. I am sure the crowds would not have flocked to him if he had kept himself to himself. His job was to do the work of Him who sent him and he was to use all the gifts and talents that he had had in bringing it about.

For me, obviously, it is fraught with danger. As a person, I love being recognised and being centre-stage, but I also hope that as a priest I will never forgot that that must never be the whole story. With being in the limelight goes a tremendous responsibility, a responsibility I sometimes find very hard to live up to.

The first piece of television training we did was a short, straight talk to camera. I had prepared my script very carefully. It had been learnt as we didn't have autocue or idiot boards. Before I had even opened my mouth I heard cries of 'stop' from the studio manager. Everyone was called into the studio and the producer was told that in no way could they put me on late at night. 'With his face on the screen,' he said, 'no one will be able to get to sleep; we've got a double for Eric Sykes.' In some way I felt honoured, as I've always enjoyed Eric's work. Mind you, I don't think Eric would be too flattered. But in another way I knew that my television career had come to an abrupt halt before it had even started.

It was also in Portsmouth that I had my first taste of journalism. On a Saturday night the *Portsmouth Evening News* ran a religious column and all the clergy of the city seemed to take it in turns to do their bit, and I was signed up for three months at the start of a new year. Here I was a little more successful than I'd been with television as not one of my articles was sent back to me, although I did think I had a bit of a cheek writing an article entitled 'How to grow old without fear' when I was just twenty-four.

Time came for me to leave St Mary's and I preached my last sermon on Whit Sunday 1965. It wasn't possible to hold back the tears. Although not everything had gone smoothly I had become very attatched to that parish and made many friends who, I am pleased to say, are still friends over twenty years later.

After packing the car I left and decided to stay for a night in a hotel, just so I could collect my thoughts before moving on to my new job. Strangely enough I stayed at a hotel in Datchet; little did I think then that I was going to spend a lot of time in that area about seven years later.

The move to the St Helier estate in South London had not been easy. The vicar I was going to, Philip Case, had been taken ill and up until the last moment I wasn't sure whether I would be able to go or not. Like St Mary's, St Peter's St Helier was a very large parish, with a daughter church called Bishop Andrewes'. It was a large GLC estate which housed people from inner-London. There were over nine thousand dwelling units (a terrible phrase), and we were slightly looked down on by the residents of the surrounding districts of Sutton and Carshalton.

The first six months in St Helier I felt very ill at ease. Like Portsea it was a training parish and the people didn't find it easy to accept someone who had been trained somewhere else. Unbeknown to the people, or my vicar, during those early months I even went off looking for other jobs but, fortunately, none of them came to anything. Another problem I found was that I was not in tune with the cockney sense of humour. It was sharper than the sort of humour I was used to and so it took a while for me to understand the parishioners, and for them to understand me.

The breakthrough came with the parish pantomime. I had been chosen to play Simple Simon – or was it Wishy-Washy? Whichever it was, it was still the part of the fool. The life of the drama group was, and still is, very strong. On the stage I could relax and be myself and gradually the dividing wall was demolished and I was very much accepted, although they did keep a very close eye on my attempts to make a bee-line for centre stage. The standard of the panto was very high and played to packed houses for all four performances.

Not all St Helier drama was pantomime. There was also the Summer Show. A fit of the giggles in the middle of rehearsals for *The Ghost Train* did not endear me to the rest of the cast, and on two occasions drama moved out of the hall and into the church: once at St Peter's and once at Bishop Andrewes'.

At St Peter's the whole parish was involved in a mystery play of the Passion. It had a cast of thousands – Cecil B. De Mille would have been jealous. It was prepared in Lent and performed in Holy Week. The commitment that people, some of whom had never acted in this sort of production before, were prepared to make was well rewarded. It also gave the audience a fresh look at the events which led up to the crucifixion of Jesus.

The other play was presented at Bishop Andrewes' Church. It was John Osborne's *Luther* and this time I was cast in the title role. If my attempt to go straight with Prospero had been a failure, here I felt I was more successful. The producer, Hilary Hunt, put a tremendous effort into the production, as she does with everything she commits herself to, and the audience responded. John Osborne has accused the Church of offering stones for bread and cliché for prophecy. This could not be said about *Luther* or about this production of his play.

I was always treated kindly in the reviews in the local papers. Actually, they couldn't have been better. Freddy Temple had always taught me to use the local paper as my parish magazine, after all it had a much larger circulation than the average parish magazine. It got to the stage where every Monday morning I would hold a telephone press conference so as to give the papers all the parish news and, what's more, they printed it faithfully.

The *St Helier Herald* was our parish magazine. It was a six-page tabloid newspaper and as well as our own church news the news of the Roman Catholic and Methodist churches was also carried, as was the local estate news. The battles with our GLC landlords featured frequently and on

one occasion a previous editor had managed to get it mentioned in the House of Commons. Second generations of families were not allowed to live on the estate, so when the son or daughter got married they had to move away. This was hurtful because, with most of the people being cockneys, they were used to keeping the family together. So under the banner headline 'One Generation Transit Camp' the *Herald* attacked this policy and even Parliament listened and, above all, acted. Half the estate was without bathrooms so once again the *Herald* campaigned. Well if cleanliness is next to godliness, then it was only right to do so.

I have never believed that the Church should not get involved in politics. For me the essential part of the Christian faith is that God became man in Jesus Christ and that, therefore, things of this world matter; without wishing to be allied to any political party, I would try to get to as many party meetings as I possibly could, especially the meetings of the Tenants' Association.

Selling the parish magazine was another matter. It was no

good just leaving it at the back of the church and hoping that it would sell itself. A bit of direct marketing was necessary. There was a faithful band of distributors but even this didn't guarantee saturation coverage. One way that ensured at least one street bought it was a feature that we called 'Down Your Way'. It featured a different street on the estate each month and the people on that street would buy it to see if anything had been written about them, but still we needed wider distribution.

A colleague of mine, Roger Tamplin, hit upon the idea of selling it in the local pubs, especially the St Helier Arms. This he did with great success and, after his departure from the parish, I decided to continue the tradition.

There was a great party atmosphere in the St Helier Arms on a Saturday night but it was in fear and trembling that I entered the Public Bar on the first Saturday of each month. I have never ceased to admire the courage of the Salvation Army and the way in which they sell their newspaper *The War Cry*. The local barrow boys, who were Arms regulars, offered to sell the paper as long as I would sing with the band. The only number that I knew which was suitable for such surroundings was Shirley Bassey's 'Big Spender' – it was one Cardiffian helping out another. How I came to learn this number I shall tell you later.

I sang 'Big Spender', the barrow boys sold the paper and, after stopping at the GLC club on the way for a repeat performance, I returned to my bed knowing that I had kept the *St Helier Herald* alive for another month. Trouble came when the people got dissatisfied with this one-hit wonder.

I had to learn another song. It was 'Love is a Many Splendoured Thing' and this was nowhere near such a success, but although I sang one or two notes flat, I am glad to say that the money kept rolling in. This was partly due to the fact that the barrow boys refused to give change.

As every clergyman knows, producing a parish magazine is a nightmare. First of all, if you can't type you have to find a willing secretary who is prepared to do it for nothing. In Portsea it was Jean, in St Helier it was Muriel. How I would have survived without their spelling, grammar and punctuation I shall never know.

The biggest fear is that you will leave out some vital information. Churches which now have weekly news-slips are on to a good thing. They can always be up to date and omissions can be made good. But with a monthly magazine you are always working a little bit behind and people are easily hurt if their piece is left out or if they have not been thanked for some gallant effort. I know that we shouldn't expect thanks, as we should be offering everything to the Lord, but thanks can be a great encouragement to us mere mortals.

Spreading the words was vital as far as St Paul was concerned and he wrote letters to all the new churches scattered around the Mediterranean and I believe that we have to continue that tradition with our magazines.

5

TO THE ENDS OF THE EARTH

At one time 'Big Spender' almost became my signature tune. If you listen carefully to the words it is not very appropriate, but as a musical number it's great fun.

I learnt it for the St Helier Hospital nurses' Christmas show. I was producing the show and we were stuck for something to close the first half. It was, I hasten to add, the nurses' suggestion that I should mime 'Big Spender' to the Shirley Bassey recording. They also insisted that I did it in drag. One of the bigger nurses was prepared to lend me her evening dress, and so I set about learning the words.

It brought the house down at every performance. I have destroyed all photographs of the performance but I was slightly alarmed when only a matter of months ago one nurse reminded me that she still had a copy!

I thoroughly enjoyed my experience as a hospital chaplain, although it is very demanding work as you move from bed, to bed, to bed. You also have to be very sensitive; some people are too ill for a visit, some people are asleep, and for some the thought of seeing a clergyman is too much to bear. After all they are generally experiencing enough suffering already without having to make polite conversation to the cloth. These people are easily spotted by the trained eye. They are either so engrossed in their newspaper that it would be a sin to disturb them or they have firmly pulled the sheets and blankets over their heads.

I also learnt right from the start that if people were in individual rooms instead of the main ward, then you told them you were on your rounds and had popped in to see them, otherwise the sight of a dog-collar made them think that the surgeons had given up.

The sight of people ill in bed used to frighten me and it certainly wasn't helped when, as a raw curate, I managed to kick over someone's saline drip. I have never liked having injections myself and the sight of others having them I find equally distressing, so you can imagine the state I was in when one mother came to me to say that her young son was in hospital and the one thing he hated was injections. She wondered if I could go and read to him at injection time to take his mind off the ensuing job. I don't know who was more frightened: the child or me. But still I was brave and this time it was my eyes that were glued to the page so that I couldn't see what was going on.

At St Helier Hospital I was able to try out my broadcasting skills. On certain nights of the week at 9.30 p.m. I did an epilogue over the hospital broadcast system. It actually went out on the same channel as the ITV sound, so I had to wait for the adverts and then jump in quickly. I knew that if I interrupted an actual programme then any hope of getting converts was doomed before I started. And what's more, temperatures and blood pressures would rise at an alarming rate.

One evening I arrived at the hospital chapel vestry exhausted. Everything seemed to have gone wrong that day; I had spent the whole time taking one pace forward and about three back and stupidly I decided to take my frustrations out on my bed-ridden congregation. 'You may think that you've had a bad day,' I started, 'but I bet it's been nothing in comparison with mine.' After I'd finished ranting and raving for three minutes I said a prayer and wished them goodnight. As I flicked the switch that restored ITV sound to their headphones, I had great pangs of guilt; here was I, meant to be strengthening the sick, and all I was doing was letting off steam. The next day I was rather sheepish as I began my ward rounds but fortunately charity got the better of those patients who listened; kindly and quietly they asked me if I was feeling better.

Christmas was always a special time in hospital. In those days they didn't try to clear the wards, so everyone was keen to see that the patients had as good a time as possible. On Christmas Eve the nurses turned their cloaks inside out and as we approached each ward the lights were dimmed so that we sang our carols by lantern and candlelight. We started at about 6 o'clock with the premature babies and ended at about 10 o'clock in the nurses' home. It was a most moving sight, especially in the children's and the women's gynaecological wards. Tears were often streaming down people's faces as they listened, once again, to the story of the miraculous birth of the babe at Bethlehem.

After the hospital visit I would nip quickly to the St Helier Arms and the GLC club to lead their carol singing, and then back to church for the midnight service. It was two o'clock before I finally got to bed and I only bothered to take off my cassock, trousers and shoes, then set the alarm for 5 a.m. because I had to be at the hospital by 5.30 a.m. for a Communion service. At 5.31 a.m. the switchboard operator from the hospital rang. She said 'Matron wants to know if anyone is coming to take the Christmas morning Communion service?' 'Tell Matron I'll be there in five minutes.' I jumped into my cassock, trousers and shoes and headed for the hospital with great haste. I think I must have travelled faster than the shepherds did to the manger, and as I arrived at the hospital Matron was waiting for me at the top of the stairs. Her look was rather severe. 'Oh Matron,' I panted, 'I thought it was Christmas Day, not Judgment Day.' With that she melted and invited me to join her for breakfast after I'd finished taking communion round the wards.

But, as with the communities, news travels fast. When I went on my rounds on Christmas afternoon I was greeted by ward sisters who said 'You're looking very fresh today, Roger. Of course, you've had a lie-in.'

One thing I did realise about hospitals was that the staff needed as much care as the patients. The demands that are put on hospital staff, whether they are porters, cleaners, sisters, matrons or surgeons, is very great and they need to be supported so that they can carry on their work. In all good hospitals they have to work as a team, each one respecting the value of everyone else.

There was one problem with St Helier Hospital. It started to sink, and this was long before there were any rationalisations or health service cuts. The foundations needed to be underpinned. One parishioner came to me in great distress and said, 'Vicar, did you know that they have opened a crematorium at the hospital?' 'Surely not,' I replied. But she was insistent, 'Yes, they have – and they have put up a board outside to advertise it.' The board actually carried the name of the firm that was doing the underpinning – Cementation! I think the lady suffered from a touch of dyslexia in the same way that I always used to think that Boots was a 'disappearing' chemist instead of a dispensing one.

For quite a lot of the time at St Helier we had been very short staffed. The vicar had left and so had some of the other curates and one of the deaconesses and there had been a nine-month interregnum. When the new vicar arrived he had a very different way of working from the way I was used to. After about a year he asked me to pop into the vicarage to see him and I thought it was to be a little chat about some parish matter, but it turned out to be something entirely different. He thought it was about time I left the parish and he would quite like to see me gone before the new curate arrived. This gave me thirteen weeks in which to find something. Industrial tribunals didn't exist in those days, so instead I turned to one of the senior clergy in the diocese, Canon Derek Tasker. He found me a temporary job as chaplain on a migrant ship to Australia. No, I wasn't being banished, it was just to give me a complete change and a little more time to find the right job.

Once again I was set to leave so many good friends, and to try and name them is invidious because I am bound to leave someone out. But I was always taught that a curate should have 'Mothers in Israel': homes I could just go to, to relax; and as the Brewers, the Lucks and the Bloomfields and many others had supplied such havens in Portsmouth, so the Hunts and the Abbotts, again along with others, had done the same in St Helier.

I left the parish on Sunday 12 May and set sail for Australia on Monday 13 May. The verger, Alec Briers, even took the trouble to have a request played for me on Radio 2 before I sailed. It's funny how my life keeps going round in circles. It was only last year that I played a record for Alec on my Radio 2 programme, *Good Morning Sunday*, to congratulate him on his twenty-five years as verger of St Peter's.

Life on the ocean waves proved to be something totally different. The excitement started with being given a first-class railway ticket; it was the first time I had travelled first class, so I could just sit and relax. Although, come to think of it, with a dog-collar on you don't need to travel first class. The moment some people see the dog-collar they pass by on the other side. Even in the most crowded trains I have had four seats to myself and all because people are afraid of travelling with a vicar.

On arrival in Southampton I caught sight of the ship that was to be my home, and the home of 1,309 happy migrants, for the next five weeks and two days. It was smaller than I expected; in fact it was much smaller. My idea of ocean-going liners starts with the QE2 and works upwards. The *Castel Felice* was the smallest ship of the Sitmar line.

The Australian government had the slightly odd rule that once a ship was carrying more than 750 passengers it had to have chaplains. I believe the National Health Service has a similar rule for full-time chaplains in their hospitals. With me there was one OPD chaplain – Other Protestant Denominations – and a Roman Catholic one, Tony Freed. The immigration department was staffed by Philippa Horne and her assistant Edith. We were fortunate as each one of us had a cabin to ourselves; the rest of the travellers were packed in like sardines. Husbands and wives had to be separated so as to get the maximum number of travellers, and they even used some cabins that were not normally used and it didn't take us long to find out why they weren't – the floors were so hot that polythene bags in suitcases stored under the bunks melted.

One of the duties of the chaplains was to interview the travellers to see why they were emigrating. This was so that the Church in Australia could welcome people into their own flocks. Something that makes me really furious is when a person gets a form that has on it a space for what religion they are. Even if they have never attended a church service, they put down 'C of E'. It would be much better if they were honest and left it blank. In a few days the OPD chaplain had finished his interviewing duties and was enjoying life with his family on the sun-deck. It wasn't that long before life had become a little easier for Tony Freed. But who was confined to his cabin for five weeks and two days? – Muggins. And just because people who never went anywhere to church decided to put 'C of E' on their application form. I asked them why they were moving to the land of opportunity, or whatever it was that I was calling Australia that day. 'It's that Barbara Castle,' answered one wife (this was when Mrs Castle was Minister for Transport). 'I went to the window, pulled back the curtains, and said "Bert, now look what that bloody woman has done outside here."' Apparently Bert did as he was told, went to the window, and looked, only to discover that there was a yellow line outside their house. After that thought-provoking discussion they were moving thirteen thousand miles, and the first thing that they saw in Sydney was double-yellow lines. No wonder they called it the Boomerang trip.

Ecumenical happenings were fairly rare in 1968, but at least Tony and I showed that we could work together even if it was only in the realm of material things. Each morning he celebrated Mass before I celebrated Communion. We both used the same altar, but as his cross and candlesticks were nicer than mine and my linen cloth was cleaner than his we decided to pool our resources. The congregation at the Sunday morning service in the bar grew as the weeks passed by and the weather got worse. It was a sure sign of God filling the gaps, and I have to admit that neither before nor since that last Sunday at sea have I never heard the hymn 'For Those in Peril on the Sea' sung with such feeling.

The voyage was hard work but it was very enjoyable. What

concerned me most was the lack of preparation that so many of the people had put into their complete change of life. Australia was welcoming almost anybody in those days, and the way they sold the country to would-be immigrants was through the weather, with the slogan 'Walk Tall Down Under'.

It was not long before the pressures began to show on the people and we were all kept very busy trying to keep spirits up and tempers down. The first port of call, Las Palmas, didn't help. People went ashore, spent money as though there were no tomorrow and then realised the goods they had bought were not quite as good as they thought they were.

To relax this tension it was decided that I should do a daily news bulletin immediately after the captain had done his 'Ship's position' for the day. I would give as many newsy items as I could gather off the short-wave radio about either Britain or Australia. I listed the forthcoming attractions that evening on board and always finished by using the slogan of the shipping line and wishing the passengers 'Yet Another Fun-Packed Day At Sea with Sitmar'. The Italian crew were thrilled to hear their line getting a name check, but the passengers let out a very audible groan.

Battling against boredom was the most demanding task. I organised a daily school for the children and this helped ease the strain a little as there were over five hundred under twelve

year olds on board. Various celebratory evenings were planned like 'Crossing the Line Night', 'Roman Night', 'Roaring Twenties Night', and they helped relieve the tension for a while and I was even able to start a world tour for my rendering of 'Big Spender'. But the thing that really took the passengers' minds off their worries were the rumours that Philippa, Edith, Tony and I used to think up most evenings at dinner.

The dinner tables were close together and people at the nearby tables always kept one ear on our table just in case they should pick up any scrap of news ahead of the rest of the travellers. So we started thinking up rumours, saying them fairly loudly, then sitting back. They travelled like wild-fire. The best rumour was that the funnel had fallen off. This had actually been a distinct possibility throughout the whole journey. Another that really got them going was that Adelaide was a request stop and unless they asked three days before they would not be allowed to get off; we were only two days off Adelaide! A bit naughty, but it kept some minds occupied for a few hours.

The first sight of Australian land was too much for both the travellers and the crew. Everyone, but everyone, rushed to the rails on the landward side. The captain sent for me to try and encourage some of the people to stand on the other side of the ship so as to redress the balance.

During the five weeks of this voyage of discovery I had combined my two strands of performer and priest in an effort to satisfy both the spiritual and emotional needs of my fellow passengers. I also hoped that I helped those people who were making such a great step in their lives to reassess their priorities.

My welcome to Australia could not have been warmer. After I had helped off-load all those who were due to settle in Western Australia, I went ashore only to hear my name being paged. I was told there were two people waiting to see me, yet at that stage I knew no one in Western Australia. The two people turned out to be the grandparents of a child whose funeral I had taken shortly before leaving the United

Kingdom. They had driven over a hundred miles to meet me and say thank you. This was an act of thoughtfulness which I have never forgotten and serves as an excellent balance to all the kicks.

I didn't actually disembark until the ship arrived in Sydney. I felt sad leaving the old *Castel Felice*, but fortunately I have kept in contact with Philippa, Tony and the children's doctor and his wife ever since. And even now I get the occasional letter which begins, 'You won't remember me, but I was on the *Castel Felice* which left Southampton on Monday 13 May . . .'

My arrival had been given a real showbiz hype by part of the media. Hearing of my antics in the ballroom each evening, some of the tabloid newspapers wanted to play it for all it was worth. It angers me still that the media continues to present a stereotyped image of the clergy. One of the Sydney papers carried the banner headline, 'Pop Priest's Life Of Parties' and the article began '"I don't sweat my guts out getting people into church," said Roger Royle, the pop priest from swinging London who arrived in Sydney today.' This was immediately picked up by one of the television stations and I was whisked across Sydney Harbour bridge to the television studios to meet one of Australia's hard-hitting interviewers Deta Cobb. I found her very pleasant and the interview certainly helped me to correct some of the false impressions given in the press.

I hope that I have sweated getting people into church, as I do believe it is very important that people should worship together, but I also believe that Christians have a responsibility to care for those outside the fold. A priest's major concern must be the offering of worship to God, but this must not be seen in narrow terms of just taking services in church and caring only for those who attend them. Giving worship to God, in my way of thinking, is giving value to the whole of His creation and its creatures and you don't respect people if you just treat them as pew-fodder.

The most memorable time of my whole stay in Australia was the fortnight I spent with a member of a religious community, called a Bush Brother, whose parish was part of the wide open spaces of the Australian outback. One Sunday I flew from Sydney to Cunnamulla in Queensland. I decided to stay in my seat the whole flight because in the newspaper that I was reading there was a story about a man who, the previous day, had been on an internal flight in America; he had gone to the lavatory and had fallen out the back door. I thought that even if I was bursting, I wasn't moving from my seat!

Cunnamulla airport was not quite of international standards. We landed on a tiny airstrip and the terminal building was a shed. I was met by the Bush Brother and we started our journey into the outback. This was the area of the Flying Doctor and the School of the Air. There was no possible chance of traffic jams, tail-backs or contra-flows, just miles and miles of space. There were also no road signs, but what worried me most was that there was no possibility of contact with the RAC or the AA, not even their Australian equivalents.

I don't think I have ever experienced such peace. I insisted that we maintain standards, so every day we stopped at 11 o'clock for coffee. You just pulled in, lit a fire, and boiled the water in the billy-can. I also learnt the meaning of the song 'A Pub with No Beer'. In the middle of our travels we came across a pub in the middle of nowhere and miles from anywhere, and I could imagine the hiatus that could have been caused if it had run out of the amber nectar. In the pub I also saw the sad side of the outback. Several stockmen had travelled from their farms, put all the money they had earned on the bar, and stayed there until they had drunk it. Not a pretty sight.

We drove through the land of dingos and kangaroos in our jeep and were made most welcome at each farm we arrived at. They didn't even mind the Bush Brother having a pommy in tow. The first job was to round up the children, but this was nowhere near as difficult as it sounds. They were keen to come to their monthly Sunday School. After the serious stuff came the fun. We had brought with us a projector and plenty of film-strip cartoons and it was my job to provide the commentary. After a fortnight I got quite good at the voices for various Walt Disney characters, but I wasn't sure that it did my voice much good. This little bit of showbiz was appreciated by young and old alike.

That night, or very early the next morning, the adults who wanted to, came to a Communion service in the farm kitchen. On one occasion it was attended by an aborigine queen of great dignity.

As we left one farm they would radio on to the next one that we were on our way. Fortunately the Bush Brother was an excellent map reader and we generally made our destination by the time we said we would. But there was one day when we nearly didn't make it at all.

I was driving the jeep and all was going well – we had stopped for coffee and enjoyed the lunch that our previous night's host had packed for us. The only real hazards on the journey were the creeks that had been dry for years. In the previous few weeks the drought had ended, the rains had come and the creeks had quickly filled up. I was driving along, chatting away, admiring the view, when suddenly I found the jeep, the Bush Brother and myself nearly engine-deep in

water. Christian charity was strained to its limits. We had to sit in the jeep for hours until the water subsided, the engine dried out, and we were able to drive on.

Wasn't I glad when we reached the farm that night. This was the most isolated farm we visited. It was worked by a young man, a twenty-four year old, who lived there alone. He had started to wonder where we had got to but quite understood when the Bush Brother explained that the pommy b****** had been doing the driving.

I was just anxious to find somewhere to lay my head, and the warning that the hut in which I was sleeping was haunted didn't really worry me. Apparently someone who had been staying there had gone out in the middle of the night and climbed the wind tower. The top swung round and cut his head off and he now haunted my hut. I was so tired I just closed my eyes and went to sleep.

Sadly, we didn't make Innamincka, the place we were heading for in South Australia. Cooper's Creek was up and it was impassable. So we returned to Cunnamulla.

This time I travelled back to Sydney by rail. It wasn't the fastest train imaginable and the heating consisted of metal hot-water bottles that were thrown in at various stops along the line. Unfortunately, the train I was on, passed the Blue Mountains at night time. Somehow this message had got through to some people who lived in the town before the Blue Mountains and they came out to the station, got me off the train, fed and watered me and put me up for the night. In the morning they got me up early, and put me back on a train that would take me through the Mountains during daylight.

I have learnt more about hospitality from the Australians than from anyone else. If you stand on your dignity you've had it, but if you are prepared to accept people as they are, you are welcomed with open arms. As long as there is enough space in their house, then you are more than welcome to stay the night. They don't make the fuss and palaver that we British often do when someone is going to pop in for a coffee, let alone stay overnight.

My return to Sydney didn't signal the end of my stay in

Australia. After a week in Canberra – a beautiful but, to my mind, a rather soulless city – I spent a fortnight in Melbourne, a city that I have now got to know very well.

6

EXCEPT THE LORD BUILD THE HOUSE

On my first visit to Melbourne I stayed with the Archbishop of Melbourne's chaplain, the Reverend Jim Grant, who himself has since become a bishop. But since then I have stayed at the home of Philippa Horne and at Caulfield Grammar School, one of Victoria's independent schools. Victoria's other independent school is Prince Charles's old school, Geelong Grammar. I have always enjoyed visiting these schools, partly because, as a visitor, you do not have anywhere near the same responsibility as a regular teacher.

It was in Melbourne that I met my first marriage celebrant, Mrs de Santis. She knew everything about showbiz. I was walking through a park on my way home when I spotted what I thought was a wedding ceremony. It was either that, or they were doing a location shot for the Australian soap *Neighbours*. I waited and it turned out to be a wedding. I stood at some distance until it was all over and then I managed to catch Mrs de Santis and ask her what she was up to. She told me that she was a licensed marriage celebrant and she would carry out weddings wherever the couple wanted. This couple had met under a particular tree in this particular park; had they met on an aircraft or on a Melbourne tram she would have been equally willing to perform the ceremony there. She came equipped with everything – rice, confetti – in fact any optional extras the couple required. Even in a busy park she was able to hold the attention of the assembled company. I didn't ask her whether she ever got requests for organs and church bells but just counted my blessings that all the weddings I took were on consecrated ground. I dread to think where I would have had to go to conduct Jan and Pete's marriage; the first time I met them was at a jumble sale at Ally Pally.

Melbourne has also become part of my speaking circuit, not just at schools and churches, but also after dinner. The first speech I made there was to launch British Airways' Superclub and celebrate the widest seats in the air. I had a great fear that the Australians would not enjoy the jokes of a plummy pommy, but as it turned out, it was a member of the British Diplomatic Corps who didn't enjoy it; but then I've never seen myself as appealing to diplomats.

The return journey to the UK was, once again, with Sitmar. It was on the slightly larger *Fair Star*, but I met an immediate snag; I had to share a cabin with an archdeacon. This I knew would do neither of us any good, so I decided to bargain: I offered to look after the children's schooling and entertainment if they would give me a single cabin. They jumped at the idea and it meant that from Auckland onwards the archdeacon and I travelled in far greater comfort.

As we made our way to Tahiti, Panama, Curaçao and Lisbon the atmosphere was far less tense. Although I was meant to be just an ordinary passenger on the return journey, I found myself helping again with the entertainment and the shipboard services. Sitting still has never been one of my characteristics, but perhaps if I had done a little more sitting and thinking I may not have got myself into so many muddles. On the other hand I would have missed many opportunities.

Within days of arriving back at Southampton I was to start work as Succentor at Southwark Cathedral. A Succentor is really an under-singer, but in my case it was really an ecclesiastical name for a dogsbody.

Southwark Cathedral was, at the time, Britain's most forward-thinking cathedral. Any thought of Barchester or a quiet cathedral close was dispelled within seconds. As I made my way, day by day, through the Borough Market to the shouts of stall-holders and market staff, I realised that there was no escaping the reality of modern life in this cathedral.

'The darts team won't be the same without the poltergeist.'

The Bishop of Southwark was Mervyn Stockwood and the Provost was Ernie Southcott. They couldn't have been more different: Ernie always wanted to be close, Mervyn preferred to remain at a distance. The line-up of Canons would have rivalled any variety bill. John Pierce-Higgins was the Vice-Provost and my nickname for him was Spooksy, as he seemed to be more in touch with the dead than the living. He was a firm believer in contact with those who had died and he was often called to exorcise both buildings and people, and on one occasion he invited me to go with him.

I was very glad that I declined his kind offer. Fighting ghosts is not exactly my scene. And what a fight it turned out to be. I can't remember whether he went armed with Bell, Book and Candle, but John set off, accompanied by a medium, to exorcise a ghost in a pub in Crucifix Lane. He believed that a ghost was someone who had not accepted that they had died. It was John's job to convince them. Somehow when I die, I don't think I shall need convincing. But this person, who turned out to be a Cavalier soldier, did. It is amazing how you can get left behind drinking in the pub, if you don't keep up with the column. Sadly, for John, this soldier turned nasty; lashed out at him and he returned to the cathedral with a nasty gash on his face. Still he was not afraid of battles. He faced many over his beliefs and doubtless he is still fighting them in heaven.

He celebrated Communion in the cathedral most Monday mornings and I would serve him. He had a fairly informal attitude towards worship. One Monday morning, for some reason, Sheila, a very faithful worshipper, was not in the congregation, so it was just John and myself. In the middle of the consecration prayer he stopped and said, 'There may be only two of us but we're surrounded.' With his contacts, I didn't know what to expect. It wouldn't have surprised me if Lancelot Andrewes, whose tomb is near the high altar, had suddenly appeared. Or if all the figures on the reredos had suddenly come to life.

The other members of the cathedral staff were just as controversial, except Frank Colquhoun and Gordon Davis. Frank was busy running the Southwark Ordination Course and collecting and composing prayers. But even he got himself into hot water once. In his Sunday morning sermon he attacked the Dean of St Paul's for indulging in stunts – he had apparently parachuted from the dome of his cathedral. I can't remember what point he was trying to prove but I think it bore some relation to Jesus and the temptations. Not only did the assembled congregation hear this attack but Frank also released a copy of his sermon to the BBC. The one o'clock news carried the story and for a while relations between St Paul's and Southwark were a little chilly to say the least.

Gordon just went about his work faithfully as diocesan missioner. Derek Tasker, the Canon in charge of post-ordination training, was a great help to me. He loved to know all that was going on at the cathedral, but he immersed himself in the training of the young clergy of the diocese and the care of his mother, and at both jobs he was excellent. For relaxation he had a great love of the theatre and it was a joy to go with him as he was so well informed.

The remaining two Canons were Eric James and Douglas Rhymes – although Douglas was not there long during my time. His books on sex were seen as being very controversial; his books on prayer were found by many to be more acceptable. I am one of the people to whom his book *Prayer in the Secular City* is dedicated. Eric has always had a very lively mind, and his sermons are still written with an economic but beautiful use of the English language. His time at the cathedral was not easy; as Precentor he was the clergyman responsible for the music at the cathedral and during his time plans were produced to make fairly basic changes. They were certainly not changes of which the lay clerks in the choir approved. Frequently after evensong on a Monday I would go to the pub with them to try and arbitrate, but it wasn't easy. However, the threatened walk-outs never happened and a lot of the trouble was caused, as is so often the case, by misunderstanding on both sides.

Although all these Canons were not residentiaries, they all had a right to have a say in the running of the cathedral, but Ernie Southcott was in overall charge. Trying to hold together this sort of team while being a definite personality in his own right was anything but easy, and it certainly wasn't Ernie's cup of tea. He worried too much about what people thought of him to be the sort of leader that the cathedral needed. At times the place was a nightmare, but at the same time it could not have been more exciting. Certainly it led the way in liturgical experimentation, and although 'Southbank religion' was often used as a term of derision, I was certainly glad to be part of it.

The regular discipline of daily worship went on week in week out, but under Ernie's guidance the cathedral Eucharist at 11 a.m. on Sunday became, and has remained, a very special service. For me, it combines the best of traditional cathedral worship with the need to share the service more with the congregation. For too long worship had been the sole prerogative of the clergy, but now lay people are reading lessons, leading the intercessions, bringing up the offertory, and even, on occasions, preaching. It has been a big step from the days when the laity were only allowed to clean the church and arrange the flowers – and be grateful that they were allowed to do that.

There were, though, two innovations which caused great stirs among the congregation. These were the Peace and 'the coffee'. At the time of the Peace two of the clergy would go down the centre aisle, shaking hands with the people at the end of each row. Nowadays this is quite common and in fact in many places it has got completely out of hand – shaking hands is one thing, love-ins are quite another.

As the clergy approached you could see the look of fear on the faces of many in the congregation. The thought of recognising the fact that there were other people worshipping God was far too much for some, especially as it involved touching someone else.

The coffee was served at the back of the cathedral at the end of the service. Again, it was too much for some, but to me it was an excellent idea. London, like many cities, can be a very lonely place and many people who attend cathedrals are lonely; to have a social gathering immediately after the service was just what was needed. After all, at one time cathedrals were marketplaces and theatres as well as places of worship, so a cup of coffee could in no way be looked on as sacrilegious. It then developed into wine and cheese receptions for events later in the day, and now it is just accepted as part of cathedral life.

Sunday choir lunch was prepared by a great team of choir mums, but sadly it had to be eaten fairly quickly. It was back to the cathedral by two for choir practice before choral cathedral Evensong. I trust that this service was enjoyed by the heavenly host as it was attended by very few human beings.

My main job after evensong was to pay the choirboys their travel expenses. As the cathedral had no choir school the boys were recruited from local schools and it was not just a matter of paying expenses; I had to check that they were continuing to pay regularly the HP on their bicycles.

At 4.30 p.m. most cathedrals either started to close down for the night or prepare for a quiet congregational nave service. Not Southwark – at 4.30 p.m. chaos ensued, for at 6.30 p.m. each week there was 'Sunday Night in Southwark'. It was an hour of non-stop, meaningful, in-depth, open-ended discussion, drama or dance, presented in a relevant way. No, that's being unfair. It was a programme with a theme which gave voice to the laity as well as the clergy, and often dealt with subjects normally left to the political parties, the newspapers, radio and television but conveniently forgotten by the Church. And what's more it was not proclaimed six feet above contradiction; by means of a roving microphone everyone had a chance to speak.

For this session all the chairs had to be moved, which was an exercise neither I nor the vergers enjoyed. A platform had to be set up, microphones and lighting arranged, and performers rehearsed. Some weeks were obviously better than others but on the whole the standard was high. It pandered to my need to be a producer, and it also delighted me that the cathedral was being used in a way that attracted quite a lot of people who normally would not have come near it. This, too, was followed by coffee and by the time that was over and, with the help of some volunteers, I had restored the cathedral to normality, I was only too pleased to return to my flat with some of the younger members of the gathering, put my feet up and enjoy a drink.

It was during my time at Southwark that I got used to planning and rehearsing big, spectacular services. All worship must be properly prepared but the 'biggies' need that little bit extra. Ernie always had great ideas, although they were not easy to put into practice. If it was a bishop's service there was no knowing what might happen. Mervyn had a great sense of theatre, but he was very unpredictable. The Southwark Ordination Service was one of tremendous dignity, but it was fraught with dangers. If anthems went on too long for Mervyn's taste, he would get restless. His chaplain and I had to stand either side of him during the service dressed in beautiful gold lamé shifts which, in the trade, are known as dalmatics. At one ordination service something irritated the bishop and it was hard for us to do anything right. At one stage he took off his mitre and handed it to his chaplain and then he thrust his crozier in the same direction but it was when he tried to get rid of his service book that I heard the chaplain snap back, 'Bishop, I can't hold any more.' With that the book was given to me. However, once the incident was over a degree of peace settled upon the proceedings.

Easter Eve could prove another difficult time. The service began in complete darkness so as to get the full effect of the lighting of the Easter candle. One year the darkness seemed to be doubly dark and suddenly in the unmistakable tones of the bishop's voice came the cry, 'I can't see where I'm going.' The Easter light came on a little early in the cathedral that year in the form of a torch as a light to lighten the bishop's way.

There was one thing that was guaranteed to bring Mervyn happiness – trumpets. A few well-chosen blasts on a trumpet were always welcome and in reality they often added a sense of grandeur to a special occasion. If it was the consecration of a bishop then the person in charge was the Archbishop of Canterbury. With Michael Ramsey in the see of Canterbury things couldn't have been easier. I even managed to persuade his legal adviser that the whole congregation should be allowed to take communion at the consecration of David Sheppard as Bishop of Woolwich rather than just a select few. It was the first time it happened and I am very pleased that it is now normal practice.

The demand for tickets for David Sheppard's consecration had been very heavy – *Woman's Own* readers wanted to see the person they read week by week, cricket supporters wanted to see their hero. When asking for tickets it was obvious that some were more used to the Oval or Lord's than cathedrals – Southwark Cathedral does not have a 'Gasometer end'!

Television also invaded the cathedral – they were recording

edited highlights. At the end of the service, just before the final blessing, they switched on all the lights and blew the cathedral fuses. When I apologised to the Archbishop about the mishap after the service, he claimed that he didn't realise that anything had happened.

Sadly, during my time at Southwark, Ernie was taken ill. Things had got too much for him. Margaret, his wife, had always been the most tremendous support to him and she needed all her wonderful resources to pull him through.

I hope that Ernie realised what wonderful things he did for that cathedral. In my position I worked closer with him than anyone and no, he wasn't always easy to work with, but he made sure that the cathedral said something new and refreshing about the gospel of Christ. His greatest weakness was his dependence on people and his inability to play ecclesiastical politics, if that can be considered a weakness. However, his contribution to the life of the cathedral must never be forgotten.

After quite a long interregnum Harold Frankham was installed as Provost. He was totally different from Ernie and during the short time that I worked with him he had the sense to sit back and listen to all the various viewpoints, and then with the support of the Cathedral Council, which was the governing body made up of the canons and representatives of the laity, he planned for the future.

As you most probably have gathered, life in Southwark was never boring. Even 'Big Spender' got another airing. It was at the diocesan clergy conference at Butlins, to which everyone was summoned and during which only a skeleton staff (if you'll pardon the expression) was left to cope with funerals and emergencies at the cathedral. During the day we conferred, but in the evening we mingled with the holiday-makers. If I'd been on holiday then, I don't think I would have been too pleased at being surrounded by five hundred clergy.

One night was 'Talent Night'; I don't think they had a knobbly knees contest while we were there. I didn't need much encouragement to enter and, of course, it had to be 'Big

Spender'. The judging was done by the amount of applause and I felt something of a cheat winning, because it was a slightly biased audience, but still the others didn't complain. However, my success was short-lived as I failed to make the national finals, but for a week or so my mind was full of those Redcoats who had made it to stardom. I wondered whether the same might happen to me – old thoughts die hard.

My talent as an entertainer was tested to the full every Boxing Day. While at the cathedral I helped the chaplain of Guy's Hospital by looking after the psychiatric clinic and the children's wards. Ann Moss was the sister in charge of the clinic and she was a regular worshipper at the cathedral and a most dedicated sister.

In that clinic I saw people come through tremendous strain and anxiety to health and wholeness. It was my first experience of people suffering from anorexia nervosa. The treatment, I thought, was often as painful as the illness.

The children's wards were supervised by Audrey Crump. She had dedicated her whole life to the care of the children. There were times when I thought she made Florence Nightingale look like an amateur. Audrey and one of the other sisters, Pam Jeffreys, invited me into the wards to say a service of blessing over the Christmas cribs. It was a beautiful part of the proper preparation for Christmas and was often a very moving act of worship. On one occasion it certainly was moving: somehow I managed, while blessing the crib, to knock over the candle, the crib caught fire and spread to the piano on which the crib was standing, and it was only the swift action of Sisters Crump and Jeffreys that saved the whole thing from turning into a tragedy.

On Boxing Day, as well as the children who were in hospital, all the previous year's patients were invited back for a party. As with all children's parties the food was demolished before you could look round. Bermondsey children don't have to be asked twice to start eating.

As soon as the tables were cleared the games began. The very sick children were carefully placed at the far end of the ward and the games had to be suitable for the children who were confined to bed, so that they could play as well. This limited the scope somewhat; musical beds was certainly out as far as Sister Crump was concerned. With the help of the nurses, and a small bottle of tonic in the sister's office (which was not available on the National Health Service), the time passed reasonably quickly, but I breathed a sigh of relief when Larry Parkes appeared. He is an excellent conjuror and gave his services free every Boxing Day.

He was allowed to get away with absolutely nothing. The children started the moment they thought he had something up his sleeve or down his sock. And it was great credit to him that at the end of a closely observed half hour he was still able to fool them. As with all children's parties the moment the children left the adults sat down, put their feet up, and breathed a sigh of relief that it was over for another year.

At times I did visit the other wards. I always found women's gynaecological wards difficult to visit because the ladies had a habit of trying to listen to what I said not only to the next door patient but also to the next door but one, and I only have a minimum of four topics of conversation: food, the family, the weather, and how long they waited for their operation. This particular morning I took a service for a few ladies – one of them, I was told, was Tommy Steele's mother, Mrs Hicks. After we'd had the short service I asked the ladies their names and when I came to Mrs Hicks I said, 'Don't you have a son by another name?' 'Oh yes,' she said, 'my Tommy.' With that the whole ward came to life. There was nothing but approval for the rock and roll star who had become a top-line family entertainer. On his way to the Palladium each day he called in at Guy's, and judging by the display in the ward he always came bearing flowers. But then, what would you expect from a Bermondsey boy?

It wasn't only in the cathedral that I had to look after the bishop. He very kindly invited me to be his chaplain on a diocesan pilgrimage to the Holy Land. I know the crusaders didn't have it easy, but there were times when I thought they must have had it easier than I had. Ron Brownrigg was the leader and we seemed to be travelling around so fast that we saw holy sights before they became holy. Ron knows the Holy Land inside out: he knows it achaeologically, historically, biblically, but above all spiritually. At his gathering cries of 'Cup, cup' the whole party rallied – including the bishop, who was fearful that he would be told off or, more important, miss further instruction.

As far as I was concerned I also enjoyed a touch of luxury as normally I travelled with the bishop in a limousine while the other pilgrims travelled in a coach. But wherever I was, I was on duty. The one day we did travel in the coach was on a visit to Masada. The day started early as we were to call in at Mamre to hear the story of Abraham, then Hebron for a look at the tombs of the patriarchs. I called the bishop early and told him that I had a flask of cold water. 'What on earth have you got that for?' said the bishop. 'Because it's going to be very hot and tiring,' I replied. 'Well, then, be sensible and for heaven's sake get the brandy.' So for the rest of the day, with the flasks of water and brandy tucked into the front pockets of my anorak, I followed him, rather like an episcopal St Bernard.

I was also set quite a difficult task during evensong at St George's Cathedral in Jerusalem. Just before the service began the bishop remembered that he had invited the archbishop in Jerusalem back for drinks after the service and had nothing with which to entertain him. So as soon as the office of evensong was over and the choir had begun the anthem I made a discreet exit. It was Friday night; the Muslim off-licences had not opened and the Jewish ones were just closing, so I had to find a Christian one. Fortunately I did so and the archbishop seemed to enjoy the evening.

It was also a deeply spiritual experience. As I wandered in the Souk I felt little had changed: there was the strong smell of spices – the same sort of smells that Jesus must have smelt – while people and donkeys hustled and bustled through the narrow and crowded streets.

On the roof of the Church of the Holy Sepulchre a group of poor orthodox monks who couldn't afford the rent for the church itself practised their faith with a simplicity of which I am sure Jesus would have approved.

Maybe the holy sights are not on the exact spot where the actual event occurred, but being human beings we need visual aids to help us in our growth of faith. The night the bishop celebrated Holy Communion in the Church of All Nations in the Garden of Gethsemane is one that will always stay with me. As I had the opportunity to pray by the side of the Rock of the Agony, it gave a new meaning to the Maundy Thursday evening Eucharist and the time that is spent at the altar of repose, where modern Christians watch and wait as Jesus asked his disciples to do when he prayed in fear.

From Jerusalem we travelled north to Galilee through unspoilt countryside, and actual religious sites lost their importance. This was the countryside through which Jesus walked and talked with his disciples. I fished in the Sea of Galilee and crossed the lake by boat and walked in the hills. In my own mind I was able to imagine the scene two thousand years ago and there was no need for shrines or churches or even marked spots.

The whole trip ended all too soon. Since then I have paid four visits to the Holy Land, always in the course of work. None of these visits has lived up to the thrill of the first one. Except for one incident: I was acting as a courier on a Christmas tour. The life of a courier has very little glamour and a lot of hard work, but there was one rewarding experience. In the small party there was a couple from Twickenham, Mr and Mrs Wells, and they were celebrating their ruby wedding. Mrs Wells had given her husband a video recorder and he was giving her the holiday of a lifetime. They appreciated everything that was done for them and they loved everything they saw. It was great to see the Holy Land through such open eyes. The most distressing thing was Christmas Eve spent in Manger Square in Bethlehem. We all had to pass through security booths on our way to the square. When I looked up into the night sky at the stars my view was blocked by soldiers armed with rifles. They were not keeping watch over their sheep by night, they were determined to keep the peace. But somehow it seemed a different sort of peace from the one promised by the Babe of Bethlehem, the Prince of Peace.

7

THE WORDS WILL BE GIVEN YOU

It was Good Friday night and I was rummaging through my flat to try and find the Christmas crib set that I had bought in Bethlehem earlier that year. What made me think of Christmas in Holy Week I have no idea. The telephone rang and it was David Jones, the senior chaplain at Eton College, suggesting that we might meet to have a chat.

The previous year I had visited Eton College, needless to say, as a stand-in. Ernie Southcott had been due to do a twenty-four-hour retreat for the boys who were to be confirmed and then the following evening preach in College Chapel. Three days before, Ernie had been taken ill, so I was sent as a replacement. It was stupid, but I was frightened of entering a world that was totally different from my own. At the time I had an MG Midget. I went to Simpsons and bought a new overcoat, so I thought the wrapping was all right, now let's sort out the contents.

The place where the retreat was held was St George's House, which is in the precincts of Windsor Castle. It was the first retreat that I had been on that was stopped for the Changing of the Guard. I had been warned not to do anything too 'way-out'; after all, Southbank religion had to be kept within bounds. The real reason was that they had had a very imaginative speaker called Robin Richardson a year or so before and he had told the boys that he wanted them to bring him something that meant something to them. The Queen lost some daffodils, British Rail lost a sign, and security at the castle lost their cool.

The ordeal was nowhere near as terrible as I expected. I am still not sure how interested they were but they were certainly polite. That evening I had dinner with the vice-chairman of the governors, the vice-provost, Fred Coleridge and his wife Julia. It was a superb meal and Fred and Julia were to become two of the people I respected most at Eton.

When I entered the pulpit I needed every bit of help I could possibly get from the Holy Spirit. I told the congregation that I knew exactly how they felt: they were expecting the Provost of Southwark and they were landed with me. It was like going to the theatre and one of those dreadful pieces of white paper falling out of the programme which says 'owing to the indisposition of Sir Laurence Olivier his part will be played by some complete unknown.'

I was asked if I would like to stay for the night and attend the Confirmation service the following morning. I felt this would be far more than I could possibly cope with, so I made some feeble excuse about being busy the next day when in fact the diary was completely clear, but I thought I had coped with the strange set-up for quite long enough.

David Jones kept in touch and I returned to Eton in my own right a couple of times to speak. When David telephoned on Good Friday night it was to arrange a meeting so that we could discuss the possibility of me becoming the first warden of the Dorney Parish–Eton College Project, hereinafter called the project.

The aim of the project was to combine the small and very beautiful parish of Dorney with Eton College. The warden would be the parish priest of the village and assistant chaplain at the college. The parish vicarage, which dated back to the fourteenth century and had actually had its longitude and latitude marked on the door-knocker, was to be converted into a conference centre. It is most probably the most worthwhile job I have ever done. Although it was hectic and sometimes the pressures became too great, I seemed to thrive on having more than one job. Clergy are renowned for wanting to be busy, it makes us feel that we are needed.

Before I could be appointed I had to be vetted, first by Eton and then by the Colonel, Philip Palmer. Colonel Palmer was patron of the living at Dorney, Lord of the Manor, vicar's warden, and the treasurer of the PCC. He was also a tremendous support to me; his death was a very sad personal loss, as was the death of his wife Frances. I could always cry on her shoulder: she was a no-nonsense lady who was very good at getting things into perspective.

The interview was unlike any I have ever experienced before, or since. We sat out in the garden at Dorney Court and the Colonel was stretched out on a long whicker chaise longue, wearing a Panama hat. Why Granada Television didn't use him as technical advisor to *Brideshead Revisited* or *The Jewel in the Crown* I shall never know. His first question was, 'Do you hunt?' My immediate reply was 'No', because it was four-legged things he was referring to rather than human souls. But hunting metaphors came easily to him.

I started my work at Dorney on 12 September, the first birthday of Ben and Kate, the twin children of David and Sue Jones. The tiny church was packed for the licensing service but there was no room for great ceremonial in this church. It had a great beauty of its own: the chancel was lit by candles and the church as a whole felt that it had been prayed in.

Needless to say, the vicarage was nowhere near ready. I had camped out in it earlier in the summer when I had taken the Southwark Cathedral choirboys for their holiday, but for three months I had to live with all the work going on around me. The garden, too, needed sorting out and I am certainly no gardener.

In all this activity I was aided and abetted by the very hard-working finance and general purpose committee. Such stalwarts as Bridget Ames, Elsie Hodges, Howard Mosley and Naomi Johnson, along with others, gave their time and their talents very generously. Working with Naomi, who was the matron in college, was an experience. She must be one of the most generous-hearted people I know. I went with her to the workshops run by the blind to buy enough bunk-beds to accommodate sixteen youngsters. They had to be bounced on and properly tested before they were bought. (Naomi doesn't believe in half measures.) We went together to a shop in Slough to buy a carpet for the conference room. It was November and Father Christmas had already arrived in his grotto. Next to him were the carpets and after looking through the sample Naomi spotted a roll of just what we wanted. The assistant was summoned and on arrival he was asked a slightly unusual question, even for a carpet salesman. 'Will it show the sick?' enquired Naomi. Having been assured that it wouldn't, we left, satisfied customers. I am not quite sure what Naomi thought was going to happen in the conference room, but the salesman was quite right: it didn't show the sick.

The first group of children who stayed at the project were from South London. The previous Sunday I had appealed in church for anyone who was free the following Wednesday morning at 9.45 a.m. to turn up at the vicarage with their car so that they could take the children to see the Changing of the Guard at Windsor Castle. Eleven cars turned up: Mrs Reffell, Mrs Loughnan and Mrs Horner were always willing volunteers. I was glad Mrs Lely didn't offer – although the children were all properly insured she had a nasty habit of shooting straight out of her garage, getting into the middle of the road, and staying there until she reached her destination. The start of one PCC meeting had to be delayed because Mrs Lely had got her car astride the new main drainage pipe. I don't know how, but we did manage to free her.

It was quite embarrassing because the children took one look at these eleven cars and decided which model they were going to patronise. Sadly, Morris Minors that had given years of service and had been treated like spoilt children were rejected in favour of newer and flashier models. But this turn-out was typical of the parish. Their faith was not a matter of hands together, eyes closed on Sunday; they put it into action by helping the less fortunate children to enjoy the countryside.

They found it hard to believe that children had never seen animals or experienced a really dark night. Through no fault of their own they didn't realise that children brought up in the inner city were never away from the sodium glare. One weekend I was without my housekeeper, Miss Tinkler (or as we called her Tinks, or Tinkerbell), because she was ill. Her cooking was marvellous and she had a wonderful way with the children. So three of the ladies of the parish volunteered to help. They were all widows, and they all knew how to deal with children. They were not quite so sure about the food, and as they stood in the kitchen – two of them still with their mink jackets on – stirring a huge pot of instant mashed potatoes and a large saucepan of baked beans, one of them was heard to say, 'I don't know how they can eat this vile industrial food.' She needn't have worried; once it was on the table it didn't linger long.

Every Sunday during term-time we held a club for children who came mainly from the Britwell estate in Slough. Youngsters from the parish and boys from Eton ran the club and it certainly dispelled any idea of Sunday being a day of rest. I wasn't altogether sure who got most out of the club. Certainly the children enjoyed themselves, but I think the Eton boys had their eyes opened. When the children returned home to Slough the young parishioners and the Etonians stayed on for tea. I thoroughly enjoyed this as it helped to break down barriers between Eton and the local community.

Independent schools, and Eton in particular, tend to be communities unto themselves. This often causes resentment and misunderstanding. When the two communities come together on an equal footing it creates, I believe, a far healthier atmosphere.

As soon as the school holiday began, we began the week-long holidays for children from the inner cities. These were staffed either by Eton boys and local parishioners or by undergraduates from universitites, especially Lincoln College, Oxford. These holidays were very worthwhile. It was only a few years ago that I was on the London Underground and saw a young black man glancing in my direction. Eventually he came across and said, 'You're that vicar from Dorney, aren't you?' He reminded me that years back he had spent a holiday at the project; now he was working for

London Regional Transport. His memories of the holiday were very happy ones.

The children arrived in groups of sixteen and I tried to have eight helpers each week. This was so that helpers could have time off, but more important than that, that any child who needed individual attention could have it. One week there was a child who adored playing chess but rarely could he find someone to play with him. At Dorney it caused no problems whatsoever.

Most of the children had never been away from home before. When they arrived they unpacked and I don't think I have ever seen so many new tubes of toothpaste in my life. Their first job was to send a postcard home. These the project provided ready stamped; telephoning was actively discouraged. Obviously there was some homesickness but it generally passed very quickly.

After tea we set out on a long walk which had two aims. First, to give the children some idea as to where they were staying. We went through the village, down to the river, along the towpath, and back, via the church and the garden of Dorney Court. Colonel Palmer's youngest son, Roger, kept a couple of wolves and it was interesting to see the children watching them. It was obvious from their nervousness that they realised that these animals were to be respected. Second, it was to tire the children out. This object was never achieved; even if we extended the walk or stopped *en route* for games, they always returned livelier than when they left. This meant that there could be near riots when they were told that it was time for bed.

Most of them were used to late nights, watching television until the white dot disappeared. But at Dorney it was very restricted. In the early days that rule caused trouble, but gradually we won through. By the time the children had gone to bed, had been told a story and, after a couple of hours, settled down all the helpers were absolutely worn out. But it was not always easy to get the helpers to go to bed either. Being students they were only too ready to talk the night away. It was only when I reminded them that they were on

breakfast duty in the morning that they thought it would be wise to get a few hours' sleep.

Outings were well planned in advance. Outings to places like Windsor Castle, the Safari Park, the model village at Beaconsfield were all regular, sure-fire successes. One outing that was fraught with danger was a trip to Burnham Beeches. These beautiful woods are still owned by the City of London and were only a twenty-minute drive from the project. There the children could really enjoy themselves without doing much harm or annoying others. The only thing that could happen was that they could lose themselves. Sometimes we had mixed feelings about finding them, but on the whole it was always the quieter ones who got lost.

I remember returning from church one Sunday to find a rather distraught Eton College master, Stephen Drew, telling me that one of the little dears had gone missing. After a detailed search and informing the police, I am pleased to say that the child was found. The news certainly brightened the strain on Stephen's face; he was a staunch supporter of the project and I was pleased to repay his support by being his best man when he got married.

Another day was spent on a local farm: one in the village

owned by Peregrine Palmer, and the other in Taplow owned by Arthur Woodley. The children certainly enjoyed these visits. I am not so certain about the animals; however, it was through one of these visits that I became a professional after-dinner speaker.

Arthur Woodley was the president of the Ayrshire Breeders' Association. A couple of years after I had left the project and was senior chaplain at Eton he telephoned me to see if I could speak at their annual dinner at a motel in Maidenhead. I felt it was a way of saying 'thank you' for all that he and his wife had done for me while I was at the project, so I accepted. The only problem was that that particular night I was rehearsing a house play at Eton. Unfortunately, I was only able to arrive in time for the coffee. On my way in to the dinner I stopped in the foyer to have my photograph taken with a cow, an Ayrshire of course, and I was soon on my feet having to face the audience.

Fortunately, the speech worked: they laughed at the jokes and were prepared to be quiet when I was saying something serious. As soon as the speech was over I had to leave to get back to Eton. On my way out I was stopped by an attractive young lady who had a voice like a duvet – it was warm and you just snuggled into it. She introduced herself as Avon Gould and told me that she worked for a consultancy, run by television personality Barbara Kelly, called Prime Performers. She asked if I would be willing to go on their books, to which I replied 'Yes'.

As I drove back to Eton my feelings were very mixed; they always are after I've made a speech. I was happy because the speech had gone well and I was very glad that I had not let down my friends, but I had those nagging doubts as to whether this was the sort of thing I should be doing. There was now an added ingredient: was it right to turn professional? I had a sneaking feeling that nothing would come of it.

I was wrong. Later that year in November I was booked by Avon to speak after a lunch at a family weekend held in Harrogate and run by the Round Table. After I had accepted the engagement I wondered what I had let myself in for. I had spoken hundreds of times at Rotary, Mothers' Union, Women's Fellowship, schools – you name it, I'd spoken there – but this was the first time I was doing it for money. I went over and over the speech in my mind until I had really learnt it. I don't use a script and I'm not even fond of notes, so it has to be learnt. Without notes or script you can keep your eyes on the audience and get a better feel as to how things are going.

Fortunately, once again I was well received but, my word, was I glad to get home. The following day I had to telephone Avon to tell her how I'd got on and she telephoned the clients for their reaction. All sides were satisfied. There were times when I wished my sermons had been subject to such scrutiny.

One effect that my after-dinner speaking has had is that I now try to preach without notes. I even find that some pulpits become an unnecessary barrier. Instead of being able to make contact with the people you are removed high above and if they are not willing to crane their necks, they gently nod off. This has nothing to do with being trendy or modern. It is just that I think the gospel of Jesus Christ is too important to be communicated in an ineffectual way. It's all very well saying that the church has used pulpits for hundreds of years, so why should a whippersnapper like me want to stop using one? I only want to stop using them when they are a barrier. The Church has to come to terms with the sophisticated way that information is now presented and understand that people are no longer trained to listen to a straightforward talk for a long time.

The after-dinner circuit is an odd one. It amazes me that companies need to look outside their own ranks for someone to entertain their guests at dinner. I realise that I am often booked as a 'funny vicar'. For some odd reason, people don't expect vicars to be funny. I hope that I don't waste the opportunity to say something serious as well, if only in the closing few minutes.

It has also taken me into a world that I had never seen before. I never knew that so much work went into promoting and marketing new brands of fertiliser or medicated dressings. And I'd never realised that dry ice and disco lights could help sell radiators.

It has also given me an insight into the strain under which some people work. Results, profit, growth, are all-important and it is no good me, as a priest, just shutting my eyes to this sort of thing. It is the world in which so many people live and the gospel of Christ must have something to say to them.

I'm not very fond of sales conferences, the atmosphere on the surface may appear very relaxed and friendly, but underneath fierce competition is raging. I am amazed at some of the remarks made by senior managers about lesser mortals and it is sad when partners are not invited to share the unashamed luxury that is being enjoyed.

For me, as a speaker, I much prefer mixed audiences. You can guarantee better behaviour. Only once has the behaviour got out of hand. It was a gathering in Nottingham and I wasn't really feeling on top form as that morning I had taken the funeral of a child. The arrival of the soup was the signal for the bread rolls to start flying through the air, and they were quickly followed by the menus which were turned into paper darts. Once the meal was over there was the dreaded loo break. Instead of the usual ten minutes it lasted a good half-hour. They returned to their tables with enough glasses of alcohol to last the rest of the evening.

The first person to speak was their local chairman. He could hardly get a word in edgeways, but it was good-humoured banter. The second speaker was a guest, like myself. He misjudged the situation entirely. It never pays to get cross with your audience and it certainly wasn't wise with this one. They decided to take him to pieces and he was only saved by the toastmaster, who realised that if this chap was to get out alive he must call a halt to the fight.

The third speaker was the national chairman and the banter became reasonably friendly again. The only trouble this time was that they knew all his stories and so finished them off in unison. It was now my turn, the hour was late, the audience wanted blood. I thought that if any blood was to be spilled it would be theirs and not mine, so I went straight into the

attack. It worked, and after a very much shortened speech I sat down to a standing ovation. This I felt was too good an opportunity to miss so I got to my feet again and told them that they had behaved so badly that I would take a collection. That night I left Nottingham with a very generous donation for the Save the Children Fund. It may have been conscience money but it was for a good cause.

At some dinners I have, obviously, offended some people. I can spot them in the audience. Some have come up to me afterwards and voiced their displeasure. I have always found their criticism hard to take, but from it I generally learn something. Certainly I prefer the criticism said to my face than to receive it second-hand.

I never thought that saying thank you to a farmer would take me into this world. Although at the moment I don't have so much time for it, and the time that I do have is often with schools and charities, I shall always be grateful for my after-dinner engagements as they kept me solvent when I was looking around for work. But even in the world of after-dinner speakers I realised that at times I'm a stand-in.

There was one frightening occasion when the telephone

rang, asking me if I would speak at a dinner in Paignton that evening. I said, 'Yes, if you can get me there.' A car was despatched; I was taken to Paddington, put on the train, changed trains at Newton Abbot, and there, on arrival at my destination, was a very smart dinner-jacketed gentleman. 'Who am I standing in for?' I enquired. 'Diana Dors,' came the reply. I suspected that I was built wrongly for that evening!

While I was at the project, life was very busy indeed. If the house wasn't full there was quite a lot of work to be done in the parish. It was about a thousand strong, but it still needed a lot of looking after. My main sources of information for visits were John and Peggy Williams at the garage. They soon told me if someone was ill or in need of help. The Palmers, too, were good at keeping me in touch. One day the Colonel telephoned to say that the roadsweeper had fallen out of bed and he thought I should know because he knew I would like to visit.

Under the direction of John Bishop the choir was revived and to the delight of the Colonel, but to the dread of the wolves, we managed to get a team together to ring the six bells. I decided that I ought to learn as well. I had never dared try the bells at St Mary's, Portsea. Although I frequently had to climb the stairs to take belfry prayers, I had never dared touch them. One mistake and I could have been in orbit, but at Dorney everything was on a much smaller scale.

Again Eton boys joined parishioners and we learnt together. I was also glad that having learnt, they didn't just ring their bells summoning others to worship and then disappear. They stayed for the service too.

Drama was even part of the life at Dorney. It wasn't Harvest Suppers or nurses' shows; this time it was nativity plays. It was very much a home-grown effort: written, produced, cast and performed in the parish. Casting a nativity play is not as easy as it sounds. There are corns which must not be trodden on and feelings which mustn't be hurt. Because Simon was excellent as the first king last year it doesn't give him an automatic right to the same part this year.

Costumes are no problem whatsoever: tin foil and wire coathangers became halos in the twinkling of an eye. And what's more, they can even make mischievous faces look angelic. Sheets and bedspreads are ideal for shepherds, and tea-towels are the ultimate in head-dresses. But the wise men need something a little more exotic. The marvellous thing about modern nativity plays is that they generally include a final scene with all the children gathering at the manger, so any left-over children can always be given a part. That has saved a lot of tears.

This particular play was going extremely well until the arrival of the second shepherd. I don't know if it was nerves or too good a tea, but as soon as he arrived he was sick all over Mary. He seemed to recover very quickly, so we didn't need to get him out; even if we had wanted to, it would have been very difficult without a major disruption. The only trouble was that the story still had a long way to go and the smell got worse and worse. Parents are very loyal to their children and the only person who really suffered was Mary. In the end it was too much for her and she burst into tears. I doubt that even Glenda Jackson has ever been put under greater strain.

8

EVEN SOLOMON IN
ALL HIS GLORY

The parish, if not the project, often provided an ideal haven
from my work at Eton College. Following Freddy Temple's
advice, I always had had 'Mothers in Israel' that I could pop
into for care, comfort and consolation.

Once I was back over the cattle grids that separated Dorney
from the rest of the world I somehow knew I was safe.
However, on occasions this wasn't altogether the truth because once back in the parish I might find that the Colonel had
embarked on another campaign on which he had decided to
enlist my help. This time it was to keep Dorney out of
Berkshire. I actually marvelled that Dorney went into the
Common Market. There were campaigns to save the primary
school, to stop 'them' digging for gravel, to replace the trees
destroyed by Dutch Elm disease; still all in all they seemed
little compared to teaching a class of fourteen year olds.

Although I had visited schools regularly throughout my
ministry, I had never faced the same class day after day, week
after week. All teachers need to be actors, if only to show
anger when things are beginning to get out of hand.

I didn't enjoy the classroom one little bit. I never had to
face the classes that some teachers did, but my heart still sank
every time I entered the room. England's battles may have
been won on the playing fields of Eton, but as far as I was
concerned they were still being fought daily in their class-
rooms.

It isn't just cigarettes that need to carry a government
health warning: young people should as well. They have the

very crafty habit of being able to smell blood and once they have the scent they go for the kill. Like any other teacher, I had to be one jump ahead. This was an extra demand on me because not all young people naturally warm to the idea of Divinity or Religious Knowledge, and as I have never seen myself, nor been seen by others, as an academic I had to draw on all my acting ability to ensure that both pupils and I survived the forty minutes. Even with academic skills some masters found it difficult to survive.

For the first lesson I didn't write a single word on the blackboard. My philosophy was that while I'm facing them I can cope, turn my back on them and there's no knowing what will happen. I tried to learn names as quickly as possible. If you are going to put someone in their place, it is so much easier if you can name them. Of course at Eton there was the added difficulty of titles, not that I bothered with them. In one class I had two earls and a viscount. I often thought that all I needed was an ace and a jack and I'd have had a poker hand. Another class made me drunk just to look at them. There was a Guinness, a Charrington, a Whitbread and a Worthington all sitting within a few feet of each other.

It wasn't just the names of the boys I had to remember – there was the Eton language itself. A term is called a half, a master a beak, a class a division, a matron a dame. Eating is called socking, the punishment book is called the bill, and they even play two games not played by any other school: the wall game, which is not particularly exciting to watch, and the field game. For a Splott lad like myself this was an added hazard. There is also a quaint tradition at Eton called capping. This stemmed from when boys wore top hats and they had to raise them to beaks; now they raise just one finger.

Apart from teaching a small class, I was also responsible for the second-year sixth form Religious Knowledge, or in Eton terms 'B-block Divinity'. This meant that two weeks out of three I had about 180 boys in the school theatre listening to an invited speaker. I hasten to add that there were other masters in the theatre; I certainly wouldn't have been left with that number of boys on my own.

Here I have to confess that I did give in to my need to be a performer. Give me a theatre and an audience – albeit a captive one – and I'm away. I certainly didn't have to wait for the lights and the make-up, or the orchestra.

I invited to speak to the boys such people as Lord Tony-pandy, Claire Rayner, Ray Buckton, Lord Trend, Anna Raeburn and many others. They were often willing to come because they wanted to take a look at the inside of this little piece of English heritage. But I decided that as most speakers were not used to talking to a group of seventeen year olds I would start the session off with an interview and then throw the whole thing open to questions.

Of course, it immediately turned into a chat show. With two chairs on the apron stage, I would begin with the immortal words, 'Hello, good morning, and welcome. My guest this morning is . . .' I knew what I was up to, the boys were certainly not easily fooled and it definitely gave me an excellent training for later life.

The other thing that played straight into my hands was 'D' worship. This was the morning assembly for the fourteen and fifteen year old boys. I am totally against euthanasia for the elderly, but there have been times when I thought it would be quite a good thing for fourteen year olds.

The rebellion of the 1960s was felt in all communities, and was certainly felt in Eton's chapels. Shuffling feet, sniffing noses and sliding kneelers are not conducive to good worship, and on top of that it was all done with an air of arrogance. Life was, to say the least, difficult.

David Jones, the then senior chaplain, or as Eton called him 'the conduct', came up with the good idea that if D block was separated from the rest it might make the worship a little easier. Eton has two chapels: College Chapel, a magnificent building built by the founder Henry VI, and Lower Chapel which was built in Victorian times when the school expanded. All the seventy collegers for whom the school was originally founded, plus the rest of the senior school, worshipped in College Chapel.

All the junior boys worshipped in Lower Chapel and poor old D were divided between the two on the basis of academic achievement, so the bright boys found themselves in the splendour of College Chapel, while those who tended to be a bit thicker were left behind in Lower Chapel. If there was any trouble in Lower Chapel, such as alarm clocks going off during the service, it was generally adorable D behind it.

Once removed to the theatre, D had to be cared for, sometimes with kid gloves, sometimes with armour plating. Such hard-working beaks as Howard Moseley, James Cook and Bryan Hooton looked after the ordering of the boys, while Anthony Bosonquet and Mike Town coped magnificently with the music. What I had to do was plan and present a fifteen-minute happening each morning. Had it been a television programme I would have had a staff of about fifteen, one for every minute, but as it was an independent school's morning worship this was out of the question. But like all democratic institutions I did have a D worship committee, but then everyone has a committee if only to look democratic.

At the age of fifteen young people are at a rather unattractive and rebellious stage. To thrust doctrine or dogma down their throats would only receive immediate throw-ups. So it was important within the planning of worship to respect and teach the fullness of the Christian gospel, but at the same time to show that the Good News is not just restricted to those things that are seen to be religious. Once again in the belief that God became man in Jesus, so D worship, rather like the *News of the World*, presented a gospel in which the whole of life was there.

The theme of the first half of D worship was based on Bertrand Russell's three aims: the longing for love, the search for knowledge, and the unbearable pity for the suffering of mankind. These titles gave me the widest scope for presentation and production. One thing that people don't realise is that the moment you leave the Prayer Book, be it 1662, 1928, Series 1, 2, 3 or 7GX, you are faced with having to devise a structure for yourself. This then means a lot of extra work and there is no chance of lifting up a book and saying 'O Lord, open thou our lips' and hoping that your request will be answered. Those people who think that new worship is just thrown together need to think again.

During the daily session, trying to make sure that all forms of presentation were used and that the best of tradition was respected was not easy. Obviously it did not meet with unanimous approval from either the beaks – who felt the moment we veered away from the 1662 Prayer Book and the Authorised Version of the Bible we were on a slippery slope to hell – or some of the young people, who could be equally traditional. I admire both the 1662 Prayer Book and the Authorised Version of the Bible very much indeed, but I do not believe that they are the final statement about matters concerning faith. And although I enjoy a 1662 Communion service, I do feel that it falls short in its lack of emphasis on Christ's resurrection.

All these services needed writing and rehearsing. Outside speakers were often invited, although not many were anxious to be there at 8.45 in the morning. Once again they were subjected to an interview so that my performing needs were met. With 250 boys in the theatre discipline was essential. As well as masters at the back, I kept a beady eye on them from the front and it wasn't long before the phrase was coined, 'the wrath of Royle'. I had no thunderbolts to hand but I could spot troublemakers at a very long range and if all were to go well it was vital that they were detected and helped back on to the right path. Some people were only too ready to say that this 'modern stuff' encouraged bad behaviour. But they had only to look at either College or Lower Chapels one morning, where everything was traditional, to know that that wasn't true.

The main use for the school theatre was, of course, drama. This well-equipped theatre, looked after most carefully by Bryan Samuel, was a joy to work in. First priority was given to school plays, but there was keen competition between the twenty-six houses to present a well-received house play. The recipe for a good house play was to have a co-operative house master, a house master's wife and a dame, and then find a producer. Then one needed to make sure that the whole house was behind the venture. Then came the dreadful task – choosing a play. In a school like Eton Shakespeare's histories are very easy to cast because you have quite a few descendants of the characters in the school. Things were nowhere near as easy with a play that I chose for Ken Spencer's house.

I have always had a great love for musicals. The first time I ever saw a revolving stage was in *White Horse Inn* at the New Theatre, Cardiff. My first visit to the West End theatre was to see *Salad Days* on my brother's twenty-first birthday. And the first time I went to the West End theatre on my own was to see *The King and I* at Drury Lane. There I was, right in the middle of the front orchestra stalls, just missing the conductor by two. I often go to the theatre on my own. It doesn't really worry me because, although I would enjoy the company of someone to comment to in the interval, in the theatre – and particularly at a musical – I am transported into a different world, and on the way home I am generally recasting and rehearsing the show, this time with someone else in the starring role – guess who!

I managed to convince both Ken and the boys that we could

be a winner if we did Sandy Wilson's *The Boyfriend*. This was certainly breaking new ground, but I always looked for enjoyment and entertainment in my productions: education came a poor third. It was the first, and as far as I know the only, all-male version of the show that has ever been produced. Casting it was difficult – I had to try and make sure that some of the 'perfect young ladies' had voices that were not likely to break in the next two months.

The music was looked after by one of the boys, Nick Earl. I had the onerous task of devising the choreography – one thing the boys were not was lovely movers. This is where I was very glad of the help of 'Mrs M'Tutor', as the house master's wife is called. Ann Spencer regularly held dancing classes in her sitting room, where some of the boys gradually realised that they hadn't got two left feet. The finished article was well worth the effort. It was received most enthusiastically by the rest of the school and even Sandy Wilson, who came to see the show, thought that in parts he enjoyed it more than Ken Russell's screen version. He omitted to add which parts.

The only other musical I produced at Eton was *Joseph and the Amazing Technicolor Dreamcoat*. This one got rave reviews, was most enjoyable to do and even resulted in an extra matinee so that younger children in the community could see it. But even this show was not without its problems. The boy playing Pharaoh got rather carried away with his pelvic thrust during the Elvis number. Certain masters felt that it was obscene and I, too, felt that he went a little too far – this from a boy who, when we started rehearsing, would hardly move his head, let alone his nether regions. Quickly one of the boys had the bright idea of sticking on the posters, 'This show is unsuitable for young children', which guaranteed a full house.

The house actually got too full. At one stage some boys would enter with their ticket, go to the lavatory, and pass the ticket out to another boy waiting outside. Sadly for one boy he passed his ticket straight into the hands of a beak and was put immediately on to the bill. Once more the posters were changed: 'This show is worth going on the bill for' – Etonians are not short of ideas for publicity.

My final offering was also musical, but this time it was on a slightly higher plane, Britten's *Noye's Fludde*. This was a combined effort with the local primary school, whose pupils played the animals. This time the musical director was Graham Smallbone, the school's director of music, or as he is called in Eton, the precentor. He is a superb person to work with. His contribution to the worship of College Chapel was outstanding and very sensitive and the only time we had a row was over Noye.

It was being performed in College Chapel and of course the orchestra was on the audience side of the performers. I wanted the performers to project their voices so that we didn't need any microphones. Graham knew that this would be impossible so, in front of the children, a battle raged. They couldn't believe their ears, although they can't have been too surprised when the victory went to Graham.

The set was devised and built by the head of the school of mechanics, or maniacs as some prefer to call it, Chris Ellis. He was very unlike the stereotype image of an Old Etonian and the ark that he built resembled something that had come out of Harland and Wolff, or Swan-Hunter Shipyards – it was huge. At one time it was thought that we would have to demolish the Chapel to get it in. Still, it had to be sturdy and it was certainly that. We did, though, have one major hitch. That was when the sun collapsed, nearly hitting a cello.

I only saw the dress rehearsal of the show but I knew that we were on to a winner. I had to leave the next morning for New York and I told the boys that I was going to negotiate for its opening on Broadway. In truth I was going for an interview about another job.

The very first house play I produced was *Seagulls over Sorrento*. This brought back many memories of the Prince of Wales Theatre, Cardiff, and Ronald Shiner. I used to take my mother to the theatre or cinema just before I returned to school, and the last thing we saw together was *The Lady-killers*, but the time before that I had taken her to see

Seagulls. I really did enjoy it, it was my sort of humour. The man sitting in front of me, however, didn't find it quite so funny. All through the first half I had been so carried away with my enjoyment that I had been kicking him. He asked if I could moderate my reactions during the second half.

Morning Departure was not such a success. One critic thought that the set was better than the production and on the whole I think he was right. The play, *The Thwarting of Baron Bollingrew*, was enjoyable, although my sympathy was with the boy who had to fly on the wire, and my prayers were for the boys who were pulling the ropes. *Under Milk Wood* was sheer delight – after I managed to persuade a couple of boys that the play was set in a Welsh village and not in Pakistan. Although one famous actor has given the impression that the accents do have something in common.

My most dramatic production was for Giles St Aubyn's house. It was John Osborne's adaptation of the Oscar Wilde story *The Picture of Dorian Gray*. Everything about this production had style, partly because no expense was spared and partly because the house was about to close and the boys were determined to go out with a bang. Their understanding and acting of the play was quite first class. I don't think that I have ever had such relaxed rehearsals. Usually during rehearsals I lost my rag at least once, but I don't think that it happened during *Dorian*. We even set a new style in Eton programmes, classy, carrying adverts, showing the early style of a boy who was eventually to become the editor of *Harpers and Queen*. I still have the silver-topped cane that was given to me as a present to remind me of that production.

One of the things that you could guarantee with the boys was that in the end they would never let you, or themselves, down. Even when rehearsals had been diabolical, somehow or other they managed to deliver the goods. It wasn't only the boys who were into drama; the beaks liked to show their talents as well. At the end of each summer half the beaks, aided and abetted by wives, dames, and other members of the Eton community, would present an entertainment. This was the only entertainment presented at the theatre by the school for which there was an admission charge. I am pleased to say that the amount raised was given to charity.

Twice I found myself producing this extravaganza. Rehearsals were not easy – disciplining your colleagues for non-attendance is not a producer's pleasantest experience but, like the boys, they too knew how to deliver the goods. The hidden acting that they did in the classroom was given full range, although to be fair they didn't have to make too much effort to be a success. Somehow people in authority making fools of themselves in front of those they normally terrorise are a sure-fire hit. *Hang on to your Heritage* was my favourite show and I even resurrected a number written by Barry Blake and Chris Peto from my days at school, as well as a routine which had been taught to me by an undertaker's daughter, an ex-Windmill girl, in my days at Portsmouth.

After three years as warden of the Eton–Dorney Project, David Jones left to become a headmaster at Bryanston School and I was offered his job as conduct. The actual appointment was quite an occasion. I had been sounded out by Michael McCrum, the headmaster, but the actual appointment was made by the provost and fellows, the governors of Eton. The provost at that time was Lord Caccia who, among other jobs, had been Britain's ambassador in Washington. Rather like the 'When did you last see your father?' routine, I was summoned to face the governing body in a magnificent room called Election Chamber. To the question of whether I was prepared to become conduct to the ancient and royal foundation, my answer was yes. There was no discussion of salary, terms or conditions. I was just taken away for a celebratory drink.

I suppose what pleased me most about getting the job was that I was the first non-Oxbridge conduct, as well as being the first conduct without a degree. I only had a diploma, a second-class honours associateship of King's College, London. It was good to feel that I was breaking new ground, because some institutions can be as exclusive as any union closed shop.

I also appreciated that I was given a free rein as conduct.

They knew what sort of commodity they were buying, and having bought me, they didn't try to change me. I saw myself as being responsible for all the worship and assemblies that took place in the school and for the pastoral care of the whole community. As with other schools, it is not just the academic staff who are responsible for its smooth running. If it wasn't for the administrative, domestic and maintenance staff, Eton would grind to a halt.

I was very well supported by the headmaster and his wife, Christine. Most Tuesdays I would have an off-the-record lunch with them, which I found invaluable. I am not sure that other school chaplains get such preferential treatment and it was on one such occasion that I broke the news to the headmaster that I had started after-dinner speaking professionally. I had been wondering whether I should tell him, and finally I had no option.

I was speaking at my first dinner in London to celebrate Robin Hobbs' of Essex fastest century in first-class cricket that season. The thought of me speaking at a cricket event with my sports record was ludicrous. One person who had been invited to the dinner was Lord Caccia, who was then chairman of the MCC. Fortunately his secretary, Ronnie, tipped me the wink so I was able to see him at the earliest opportunity. He was pleased – he would encourage any sort of private enterprise as long as it was legal. I wasn't sure it would be so easy with Michael so as we walked back from the dining room to the drawing room I said that I didn't know whether he had heard that I had started to do some after-dinner speaking. 'Yes,' he replied, 'We have heard, and we were shocked.' Fortunately Christine came to my rescue. 'What do you mean we were shocked? I was pleased and you were jealous!' The matter was discussed no further. It was great, however, to be able to discuss matters informally, and a privilege I hope I never took for granted.

I also had a weekly meeting with either the vice-provost or the provost, Lord Charteris, ostensibly to sort out the chapel notice sheet, which was called the chapel bill. But it was also an invaluable time to sort out other things and air ideas. Lord

Charteris has a way of being able to diffuse things which may appear extremely difficult, but I suppose you can't be the Queen's private secretary for over twenty years without being able to sort out the important items from what can be dismissed.

Of all the services that I was responsible for, it was the Holy Communion service in College Chapel on Wednesday evenings that I most enjoyed. In the quietness of the subdued lighting of the ante-chapel a good number of boys, and some masters, would attend this voluntary service. All the other chapels and assemblies were compulsory, so the atmosphere at this service was very relaxed. Only those who wanted to be there attended. And then they were invited to my house for coffee, a general chat, Bible study, or to listen to a speaker.

I was also thrilled that during my time at Eton there was the first celebration since the Reformation of a Roman Catholic Mass in College Chapel. We celebrated Communion in the ante-chapel, so the Roman Catholics said Mass in one of the side chapels. We then came together for coffee. I must say that the divisions in the Church have brought me great sadness. Whenever I am abroad I don't search for a Church of England church, I go to the church of that country. I feel that it is the divisions within the Church that weaken the witness of the gospel. It is very difficult, I believe, to preach peace when we are at war with one another.

My biggest failure at Eton was the standard of confirmation preparation. The numbers were large and there was a tendency for boys to get 'done' because it was convenient. Sadly integrity went out of the window, and boys who would have protested if other demands had been made upon them, 'got fell in' as regards confirmation. Some had even been promised a case of port if they got confirmed. The numbers I had to prepare were big and I was often doing as many as nine confirmation classes a week, and although I tried to write to all their home vicars there was often very little link with the local parish. I had the slightly grim feeling that they were joining yet another Old Etonian Club.

I was very glad that just before my time as conduct the

confirmation and first Communion services were combined. Before, it had meant that we had to have two services, or as Lord Caccia had put it, two bites at the cherry. Now it did mean that all the boys made their Communion at least once. In the days when the Communion and confirmation were separate there were some who didn't even get as far as their first Communion.

The problem with independent school worship is that it is far removed from what is experienced in many a parish. At Eton we could have the best of everything. Vergers and cleaners kept the Chapels clean and tidy, the flowers were always glorious, the music superb and the sermons, on the whole, geared to them. They didn't have to worry if the roof was falling in or the heating failing. Nor was there any concern as regards committed giving as far as the collection was concerned. The chapel collections always went to charities. If the charity appealed to them, they generally gave more. When it was discovered that there were some magnificent medieval wall paintings behind some panelling, the panels were removed and the paintings restored. No jumble sales had to be held, nor was a fund-raising thermometer placed outside the chapel. Because King's College, Cambridge, Eton's sister foundation, had Rubens' *The Adoration of the Magi*, someone gave Eton one.

Fortunately a number of Etonians realised what a rarefied atmosphere they lived and worshipped in and they didn't expect the same unashamed luxury from their own local community. But the others sadly gave up, apart from attendance at memorial services and other occasions of obligation.

9

SUFFER THE LITTLE CHILDREN

Eton can become a totally absorbing and very demanding community. It is also a transitory community. There is a five-yearly turnover; boys who arrive in a somewhat nervous state leave as very self-assured gentlemen. When they leave the boys have a very pleasant custom of giving photographs of themselves to those members of staff who have meant something to them. Over the years I have built up quite a rogues' gallery. The photos varied from rather formal portraits to very off-beat symbolic representations. Sometimes they were just signed by the boy and sometimes the boy wrote a report on your work. One grandson of a very well-known politician put that I would have got on a little better with him had I taken more time to understand him. Sometimes the boy expresses his thanks for something you have done. I think the best one I received was from a lad who was often on the edge of being on the wrong side of the law, who wrote, 'Normally I wouldn't, but on this occasion I think I might, thanks a bunch Rog.'

These 'leavers' as they are called were generally prominently displayed on masters' mantelpieces. In fact there was quite a competition between different masters to see who was the most loved.

When masters leave they don't issue photographs. Actually, come to think of it, some masters never leave. Certainly deciding to leave Eton is not an easy decision to make. I knew it had to be made. I don't believe that school chaplains should settle in for life, as it is only too easy to lose touch with the outside world, let alone the outside church. I had no idea what

I wanted to do, although I was fairly sure that I didn't want to return to ordinary parish life.

The thought of trying to get into the media was, of course, strong. But I felt it was a little unreal. Any showbiz person such as Penelope Keith, Reginald Bosanquet or Elton John who came to Eton was generally, at some time, entertained by me. I seized the opportunity to bend their ear. London Weekend Television made a programme based on a book called *The Treasures of Eton* and the production staff made my house their home. Producer/director Bryan Izzard, presenter Russell Harty, and production assistant Tanya Bruce Lockhart, all whetted my appetite for the glare of the lights and the stare of the camera. But being involved in a one-off programme and actually earning your living from television are two totally different things.

One thing I had to learn was that off-the-cuff remarks like, 'You would be marvellous on television' do not constitute a firm contract. The knocking on doors has to go on. But the knocking became a little more frantic when I realised that I had to get a job.

My decision to leave Eton was taken while driving along the M4 from Bristol back to Eton. I had been to a memorial Eucharist for Derek Tasker in his old parish in Bristol. Although I had been close to Derek during my time at Southwark, I had not heard of his sudden death at Eastertime, so I missed the funeral. Having heard that there was a service at Bristol, I thought the least I could do was to go there, if just to say thank you. For some reason I felt very down during the service; it was another friend who had gone. So my drive back to Eton was spent thinking out the future. I thought I had been at Eton long enough; it was time to move. When I returned I handed in my notice. Both the provost and the headmaster expressed their regrets and both were prepared to help me look for a new job. But what job?

I contacted my old boss, the Bishop of Southwark, who invited me for lunch and just before the other guests arrived he walked me round the garden for eight minutes. He said he was afraid that he had nothing to offer me and suggested that I got in touch with the Clergy Appointments Secretary, but this also proved to be a rather fruitless visit. The actual interview didn't get off to a terribly good start when, before any form was filled in or discussion held, the secretary said to me, 'What about Great Yarmouth?', to which I replied, 'For a summer season or a longer run?' I realised that the reply was facetious, but it just seemed as though any place was being pulled out of the hat. I didn't know Great Yarmouth and they certainly didn't know me. I then had to fill in a form which, looking back on it, I now realise was necessary, but at the time it made me very angry. The form shows the Church of England at its most ridiculous. I can't remember it clearly now, but it seemed to concentrate on what ecclesiastical outfits I was prepared to wear and where I preferred to stand at the altar, rather than on an assessment as to how the guidance of the Holy Spirit should be sought to plan my future ministry.

It may be that I was expecting too much, but I did just hope that with my experience of parishes, hospitals, cathedrals and schools, there would be some suitable niche for me. But I also recognise that at the same time I was sending out signals that I really did want a job in the media.

I was offered one parish, just off the A1, and the patron and churchwardens could not have been more welcoming. But I wasn't sure that I could commit myself to it in the way that a parish priest should. Another possibly exciting offer had also come my way. John and Candis Roberts, two friends of mine at Eton, had suggested my name to someone who was looking for a headmaster for a top prep school in New York, St Bernard's.

I was seen, first of all, in London and seemed to pass the test. I think I impressed the interviewer with the fact that I had to leave early so that I could be at a reception at St James's Palace. Well, I suppose it does sound a little more impressive than saying you have to catch the last bus home. I was then invited to go to New York for a more detailed interview and a chance to see the place. I flew out after the first dress rehearsal of *Noye's Fludde* and for the first time I travelled in a class other than what is affectionately called 'cattle class'. I got a taxi from JFK Airport to Manhattan and was cheated by the taxi driver. I think he charged me more than double. When I arrived at the school I was met by one of the trustees and from then on it was non-stop interviews.

Wherever I went, except to the lavatory or bed, someone went with me. Not even a taxi ride was a breather between interviews, someone travelled with me and the interview continued. I had to teach a class of the senior boys, fourteen year olds, and I seemed to get on quite well with them. But the timing of the lesson was carefully staged so that after it was over the boys could get home quickly, tell their parents what they thought of me, and then the parents were invited to meet me later that evening so they could make their own assessment.

Exhausted, I caught the Saturday morning flight to London and arrived back in time to conduct the Remembrance Day service at Eton. Between then and the middle of December I had several calls from New York, but it wasn't until December 15 that I was actually offered the job. The offer was by telephone and I didn't accept it immediately but asked for details to be sent to me in writing. That, I thought, would delay things for at least a week and possibly, with the Christmas rush, a good deal longer. But I hadn't reckoned with telexes. At that time they were not part of my world. That morning a telex arrived, I was offered the job, and the terms and conditions would have put me in a financial league that I'd never even dreamt of.

That night the telephone rang, it was New York. They said they had done a silly thing. They had let out that I had accepted and I stupidly said, 'Well, then I accept.' Having said that, I even put my acceptance in writing. At many times in my life I have acted first and thought later. After the euphoria of being accepted and getting the job I began to think seriously about what I had committed myself to.

A couple of days later one of the trustees flew into Heathrow. I met him and took him home to Eton. As I heard more

about the job and the discussion that had led to my appointment I began to feel uneasy about my hasty acceptance. On
the Friday evening I was at a dinner party at Mervyn Stockwood's. The former Bishop of Woolwich, John Robinson,
was also there and I told him about my doubts. He thought I
should go ahead, that I would enjoy the experience of
America, but I still felt uneasy.

I telephoned a former parishioner, Tony Bonvoison, and
asked him if he could drop everything and come and see me.
He did, he listened, he asked questions, and for the first time I
looked objectively at what I was about to take on. At the end
of what was a heart-searching session I realised that I had
gone after the job for all the wrong reasons. I had been fearful
that I would be out of work, and the thought of working in
New York had a certain kudos value and glitter about it. But I
never wanted to be a headmaster and I realised that one of the
reasons I was attracted to the job was because an Englishman
in New York might have a stronger chance of getting a job on
television. I also realised that the school wanted me more for
PR than as a headmaster and this I thought would cause
difficulties. I shall always be grateful to Tony for taking the
trouble to listen and for helping me think through what had
become a very complicated situation.

On the day after Boxing Day I travelled down to Salisbury
and saw the Dean, Sydney Evans. I told him what I had told
Tony and he said, 'What you are saying is that you have made
a mistake and you don't want to go.' I agreed, so he said there
was only one thing left to do and that was to send a cable to
New York. I went straight to the Post Office in Salisbury and
did the deed. Breathing a sigh of relief, I travelled on to my
little bolt-hole in Sherborne. But I breathed too easily: New
Yorkers don't give up that easily.

For the next ten nights I had telephone calls from New
York. I even had a visit from the trustee I had met at
Heathrow. Their final act was to get an Old Etonian parent to
invite me to the Garrick Club to apply pressure on me to
change my mind. He didn't succeed, but I felt very grim. He
suggested that I at least went over to America to explain

myself. Fortunately Michael McCrum came to my rescue. He said he wouldn't allow me to go in term time and so I returned to bed, sick.

In the meantime I had given up the chance of another job. I had applied to BBC Radio's Religious Department for a job. I had been shortlisted but had withdrawn my application, thinking that I was on my way to the Big Apple. God moves in a mysterious way.

With two terms to go I was without a job, but there was a glimmer of light coming from the media world. Christopher Martin, the then head of the Independent Broadcasting Authority's Religious Department, had been very kind and had introduced me to John Barton, the religious adviser to Southern Television. He invited me to do a couple of epilogues for Southern. They went well and suddenly I found myself becoming a regular contributor. I wasn't exactly peak viewing, as I reckoned that on a good night the programme was watched by two cats and a budgie, but it was a toe in the door. Actually I found out later that one of the main groups of viewers for the epilogue were publicans. They had their sets on as they washed up the glasses and put away the empties.

I thoroughly enjoyed recording the epilogues. There was a great team who used to meet in a tiny studio, which I affectionately called "the broom cupboard", on a Monday afternoon in Dover. We started at 2.30 and with luck I caught the 4.40 train back to London. All seven nights were recorded in one fell swoop. It was sometimes difficult remembering which night of the week it was, but I always finished with, 'Good night, God bless, sleep well.' There was no such thing as a script going up in the lens, or even idiot boards, and I used to maintain that the cameras were kick-started – but the atmosphere could not have been better.

John Barton took great trouble to provide variety and it was very encouraging to know that his efforts were rewarded. I was asked to do the very last epilogue for Southern before they lost their franchise and handed over to TVS. I did it on a theme which I thought was very appropriate, 'Big Farewells from the Bible'. I felt that Southern Television was a little like Moses: it had seen the promised land, but it hadn't quite made it.

Anglia Television also invited me to do their epilogues. This time it was the fatherly eye of Peter Freeman and his secretary Ann Rudland who kept me on the straight and narrow. It also involved a lovely day in the city of Norwich. But even with those two companies, whose service to religious television has always been generous, I came across the thing that I dread: the putting of religion into a pigeon-hole. Soft blue backgrounds, stained-glass windows, big leather chairs, were all seen as being part of the essential scene. I realise cooking programmes have to follow a set pattern, but I do think that a lot of harm is done to the gospel by trying to present it in a fixed and rigid way. The image it gives is often out of date and just convinces people that religion and faith deal with the past or are just for the elderly.

My link with Southern was to prove a lifeline. By the time the summer term had ended at Eton I was still without a job. The final leaving had been very difficult; I was both tired and emotional. Eton very kindly gave me £1,500 to see me through the next few months so that I could use them as a sabbatical, a period for reading and recharging the batteries. It was generous, but it didn't make up for the fact that there was no job in the pipeline.

I based myself in Sherborne, although for three months the Provost of Southwark kindly allowed me to use a spare flat belonging to the cathedral as a London base. But just at the time I got a job in London the cathedral wanted their flat back. Hunting for a home in London is not easy, but thanks to a contact with the Church Commissioners I managed to get a bedsit on one of their estates on the edge of Brixton. It was quite a culture shock, moving from a five-bedroom, two-bathroom house in Eton to a bedsit in Brixton. I could have fitted the whole of the bedsit – bathroom, kitchen and all – into the sitting room of my Eton home. Most of my furniture I stored in one of Eton's atomic fallout shelters.

This whole period was certainly a change of life as far as I was concerned and I have now become a great believer in the male menopause. The job I managed to get in London was with Save the Children. Eton had forwarded to me an invitation to attend the launch of Save the Children's Stop Polio campaign. As well as accepting the invitation I asked whether there were any jobs going. I was fortunate, there was one that had just been advertised. It was as promoter of the Stop Polio campaign. It was basically a fund-raising, public relations job. I knew little about polio but I was sure I could learn. I was shortlisted and got the job. After the interview my new immediate boss, David Creedy, invited me home for a meal to meet his wife, with the kind words, 'Welcome to your new career.'

I don't think that I have ever really thought of life as a career; I am also not sure that I have been willing to put my life entirely at God's disposal. But I have tried to work where I have thought that I have had something to offer. I have never played the church career-structure game, because to play it properly you have to be prepared to serve on the committees of the Church, which are endless. And if there is one thing I find difficult, it is committees – in large ones I tend to behave rather badly. I also realise that I have wanted the

Church on my terms and this may well have caused resentment. Where it has, I think there has been misunderstanding on both sides.

The job with Save the Children was interesting to begin with. I found being office-based difficult, and I also didn't find it easy to adapt to the pace at which charities often work. I tend to be a get up and do person, whereas often with charities i's have to be dotted and t's crossed before new work is embarked upon. Also, my position in the charity was quite junior, so I couldn't really expect my ideas to carry tremendous weight. It wasn't long, however, before I was put on the campaign trail. Armed with an excellent set of slides and information prepared for me by the Stop Polio doctor I travelled the length and breadth of the country – if it was Wednesday it must be Belfast. I spoke to supporters of Save the Children, Women's Institute, Rotary, Mother's Union, Round Table, in fact wherever two or three were gathered together I would put up a screen, set up a projector and talk. Obviously, once again, the performer in me was being kept happy.

I knew the talk backwards. Supporters of Save the Children treated me generously – and gently. Some of the schools I visited were slightly more challenging and my experience at Eton certainly came in handy, although I still faced large assemblies of youngsters with fear and trepidation. There were times when I got rather cross, usually when I realised that some schools were using me to fill in the last afternoon period so that the members of staff could have a slightly gentler end to the day. I got over this by asking a number of staff to stay with me in the classroom. On the whole I thoroughly enjoyed these visits, especially as I learnt more about the strengths and strains of the maintained system, and I hope that I never took the generosity of these schools for granted.

The talk took on renewed fervour after I paid a visit to Malawi, one of the countries in which the Stop Polio campaign had begun. It was a great eye-opener. Preventative medicine is, of course, the cheapest sort of medical care. We take it for granted, but in the developing world it is by no means automatic. You have, first of all, to get the co-operation of the country. The days are gone, I am glad to say, when you could sweep into a country and say that you have come to do them good.

In some areas this means being sensitive to the fact that witch doctors and medicine men still exist. I remember one Saturday I was in Blantyre in Malawi and I took a trip to the local market. As I wandered among the colourful stalls selling anything from fruit to household goods I came across a medicine man. His stall was certainly colourful: he had an array of twenty bottles, all lined up, all containing different coloured liquids. I told him I had a headache and I needed a cure. Pointing to the bottles he said, 'You try.' I did. They all seemed to have a gin base so I didn't try many in case my headache got worse. But what struck me was that as well as offering you medicine he was also prepared to mend your bicycle. I thought, if only doctors in Britain were prepared to do this it could end any possible strain on the NHS!

Local communities also had to be convinced that preventative medicine was a good thing, so local chiefs had to be sought out. Once you had got their approval you could go ahead. However, it was anything but plain sailing. This particular polio vaccine was intended to be given on a sugar lump and had to be given three times to ensure complete protection. The vaccinating team would arrive at the village having sent warning the previous day that they were on their way. A central point would make an excellent clinic and generally by the time the team arrived there was an orderly queue waiting. The vaccinators didn't have to be highly trained as with this vaccine no needles were needed. It was just a matter of having good eyes and knowing where the mouth was. Even I was allowed to administer the miracle drops. The mothers stood in a line with their babies strapped to their backs and the vaccinators went along the line, squeezing the cheeks of the children so as to put the drops into their open mouths. By the end of the exercise, the noise of the crying children had reached crescendo point. They didn't take kindly to the bitter taste but sadly for them there were no sugar lumps.

Some mothers got the idea that if three doses did good, seven or eight would protect you from everything. So a careful check had to be kept on who got what. Mothers were even prepared to nip across the Mozambique border on a sort of medical awayday so as to get their children vaccinated. I had the chance to see the beauty of Malawi, to bathe in the lake, and to realise that although we may have a lot to offer the developing world, the developing world still has a lot to teach us.

One Sunday morning I went to one of the local churches for Communion. It was packed and there was certainly no chance of hiding behind a pillar, hoping not to be seen, in order to enjoy a quiet private word with God. I was made most welcome and the worship was, to say the least, lively. When it was time to receive communion the adults went up first, and as soon as they had received it, the children tore through the church to get their blessing. They came back to their parents touching their heads and trying to feel the blessing or to check whether it had taken. From the glint in their eyes it looked as though there was still quite a lot of Old Nick left in them.

My travels took me also to Swaziland and Zimbabwe. In Zimbabwe I met a marvellous Save the Children nurse called Dora. She was from Northern Ireland, trained in Scotland, and had a wonderful way with the mothers and their children. Her main form of communication was a smile or a touch – Dora wasn't too good at foreign languages. She and her nursing colleague said that I could stay with them in the medical encampment in the Zambezi valley area. I arrived early in the afternoon, Dora showed me to my room, and then asked me if I would mind if we had our evening meal early. It really didn't worry me what time we had our meal, but the reason for its timing did interest me: the cook needed to get home before the elephants arrived at the river.

I was to meet up with Dora again when I went out to the Sudan to make a film for Save the Children on their work with refugees. I teamed up with a freelance cameraman, Eric Thirer, and together we made a twenty-six-minute documentary. Eric couldn't have been easier to work with and his expertise certainly made up for my inexperience.

Getting to Gedaref had not been easy. The bus takes about six hours from Khartoum and you tend to feel every bump in the road, so I was glad to arrive at the Save the Children house. There were Dora, another nurse called Dorothy and the doctor, an Australian, Kim Mulholland. Wherever Dora is, there is a pot of tea. She can make it in the most difficult circumstances and I think if she were ever to be invited on to *Desert Island Discs* I am sure the luxury she would take with her would be a limitless supply of tea.

I didn't know what to expect as I had never seen a refugee camp. This one was very neat. Row upon row of smart little tukels, cleverly made homes of wood, thatch and mud. The mothers were kept busy caring for the family and their temporary home. The children either played or went to a little school. The men just waited; there was nothing for them to do. The water was brought to the camp by lorry and the health care was supplied by charities. The thing that struck me was the tremendous courage of the refugees. Sudan had five million; a lot came from Ethiopia. One lad that I met had found his best friend with his throat cut lying on his doorstep with a warning that the same thing would happen to him if he didn't clear out or change his ways. He chose to clear out even though it meant a difficult and dangerous journey and a very uncertain future.

One of the scenes that we filmed was Dora making a home visit to a tukal to visit a newly-born baby and her mother. For the visit Dora took an interpreter. As we moved into the tukal *en bloc* it all became too much for Grandma in the corner and she fainted. Dora had to revive Gran before she could start caring for the new life.

I think my greatest contribution to international understanding came on a visit to India. Here again I was seeing the work done by Save the Children and I was particularly impressed by an organisation called Artik Smata Mandal – an atheist organisation which couldn't have made this Christian more welcome. They supported and encouraged development in about twenty-five small Indian communities. I was taken around to see what they were up to. They were helping with the health care of the people – helping them to develop the land and to set up things like fish farms. They were also keen to see that the young, the up and coming generation, were properly educated. Wherever I went I would visit schools, and the one thing that I could be certain of, was that the school would lay on an entertainment in the form of a traditional dancing display.

Obviously when it was over I could show my appreciation by my smile and applause, but I thought I really ought to offer them a little bit more. So I taught them the Hokey Cokey and they caught on fast. I felt that I had done my bit for peace and understanding.

That understanding nearly broke down when one of the hotels that I stayed in seemed to have a curious plumbing system. I was thrilled to find that I had a shower and loo *en suite*. I didn't expect it as I was only paying £5 all-in per day. But I wasn't quite so thrilled when I found that every time I flushed the loo the shower started, and when I turned on the shower the loo flushed. However, I was not prepared to let a little thing like that cause an international incident.

10

THROUGH A GLASS, DARKLY

Even with a renewed vision gained by having seen a lot of the work of Save the Children both abroad and in this country, the job was not making enough demands on me. I was touring the country, spending a tremendous amount of time travelling, and delivering basically the same speech. This, I thought, was a waste of Save the Children's money and my time. So I asked them if I could become a part-timer. By this I felt that everyone would benefit.

Once again the pressure was on to find more work and, once again, I looked towards television. By this time I had to re-establish ecclesiastical roots. The Reverend Dominic Walker was the rector of St Mary Newington, a parish near the Elephant and Castle, and he asked me if I would like to join the staff as an honorary curate. For this suggestion I was very grateful. The parish is a very lively one. Its worship is strong and its congregation committed and friendly. I so appreciated the sense of belonging that being attached to St Mary's gave me. Although I was not there every week, I felt that when I returned I was always welcome and when I was away there was a strong core of people who remembered me in their prayers.

I suppose I only realised this fully when there was a change of incumbent. Dominic left to become the vicar of Brighton and it was obvious fairly quickly that I didn't really fit in with the new management. Admittedly it was more difficult as I was away more often. But when the break came I realised that I had lost that strong sense of support and belonging. I needed that parish far more than it needed me.

However many times I curse the telephone for interrupting

me, there are times when I realise what a blessing it is. The telephone rang and it was Southern Television asking me if I would appear on a chat show hosted by a weather man, Trevor Baker. It was produced by Bryan Izzard. Trevor was to interview me about the epilogues and my work as an after-dinner speaker. The other guests were Rita Webb, Arthur Mullard and Cardew Robinson, so you can imagine that it was a fairly lively gathering – and aitches were dropped all over the place.

The interview went well; afterwards I chatted with Sidney Perry, one of the top programme planning men at Southern. He asked me if I had any ideas for a religious television series. I said that I had. I wanted to do one which had a sense of humour. My faith is based on the resurrection of Jesus Christ, yet I think that sometimes, the way in which the gospel is put across, it seems to be fixed in the sorrow and guilt of the crucifixion.

I was given Bryan Izzard as my producer to think something through and come up with a pilot programme. This was right up Bryan's street. He is nothing if not flamboyant and the chance of making a religious programme with a bit of showbiz razzmatazz seemed to suit him down to the ground. It was decided, very wisely, that this should not be a one-man show. The author and broadcaster Mary Craig, whose book *Blessings* is one of the most moving stories I have ever read, joined me. She acted as an excellent balance to me. Someone had to have their feet on the ground. And so that there was a younger interest in the programme, the music was supplied by Garth Hewitt and the roving reporter was Sarah Kennedy. It was a great team and we seemed to support one another. Sarah, who had more experience of television than the rest of us put together, was extremely patient with those of us who were using autocue for the first time.

Before the programme actually reached the viewing public we made two pilot programmes. On the tickets for one of these programmes the show was called *The Royle Variety Show*, but by the time it was networked it was called *Royle Progress*.

127

It had everything: a signature tune composed and recorded by the Swingle Singers, under the expert eye of Harry Rabinowitz; three sets; parachuting nuns; Cliff Richard; Yousuf Islam; a priest who made train noises; and a wrestling Methodist minister. I played snooker with Terry Griffiths and beat him hollow, thanks to trick photography; I enquired into the tourist trade of Buckfast Abbey; and I interviewed such people as Beryl Reid, Richard Ingrams and Willy Rushton. Music wasn't just the upbeat, up-tempo sound of Garth. Mrs Rosalind Runcie was prepared to tickle the ivories, although that was not without its dangers. The piece she chose to play was 'Gollywog Cakewalk', not a piece that would be approved of by certain sections of the Race Relations Committee. However, Bishop White, who was the black Pentecostal bishop for a church in Lewisham, treated it as a matter of great fun. Researchers Kevin and Jennie looked everywhere for stories.

We had also a live audience. Religious shows, if they have anything, tend to have a congregation – but this was definitely an audience. The programme got mixed reviews. There were some people who loved it, while others found it most distasteful.

It was certainly launched in style. *Royle Progress* was not to be a quiet hole in the corner affair with a preview being given in some tiny television theatre in an inaccessible part of London. No, Izzard thinks big. I was flown to Montreux, and the programme was launched at the celebrated television festival. I gave my first interview about the programme to a *Daily Mirror* journalist on Geneva railway station. I did not really know what had hit me, nor did some of the press. They are fine when religion is confined to hymn-singing, but once it steps outside those confines they don't always know how to cope. Some of the newspaper reports which suggested that I was going to ridicule the Church were far off the mark. But at least they did show an interest in the programme.

It ran for six weeks and by the end of the run I was, I believe, beginning to settle down and say something worthwhile. Certainly the director, Dave Pick, had worked extremely hard to get the right balance between fun and serious content. But trying to break new ground is always difficult, and I remember that we did strive to be different. At one dress rehearsal Bryan called me into the control room and said, 'Darling you're interpluggable with fifty-seven other presenters, we didn't book you for that, did we?' I was sent away to think about it.

Having stepped out of the traditional line, I realised I was very exposed. I have never taken criticism easily and I must say that some of the letters I received were extremely hard to take – I still find them so. It was glorious reading the ones that said that the programme was marvellous and I was wonderful, but it was the ones that tore me and the programme apart that really stuck in my mind.

When people disagree with a programme or a presenter, they have every right to put their point of view, but sadly the criticism often becomes personal abuse. And certainly Christians are in the forefront of this. If a letter was signed, 'Your sincere friend in Christ' I often knew that the attack was going to be strong, to say the least. One such letter, when it had run out of abuse about the programme, added, 'And what's more your ears stick out.' Now I know that – they have stuck out for the past forty-eight years, and as a child I was often teased about them – but I have never thought that saying my ears stuck out could ever be regarded as part of constructive criticism.

The press were mixed in their reviews. TV critic Maggie Forward thought that I was a bit of a twit and the *Daily Mail* features writer, Simon Kindersley, felt that I had missed the target, and to back this up he quoted low viewing figures in the middle of the series. For me the sad thing was that we didn't get the chance of another series. With Southern losing the franchise, no one else seemed willing to take it on. Yorkshire Television, which might have been the most suitable home for it, was already planning a similar series with Frank Topping, so there was no place for it there. However, it didn't die entirely. Good old Ulster Television, based in Belfast, was willing to give it a go. As you can imagine, doing a religious programme with humour in Belfast was not easy, and I respect Ulster Television for taking the challenge. Producer Andy Crockart was certainly up to it.

I really enjoyed my visits to Belfast. I generally stayed in the Forum Hotel, then called the Europa. It had the dubious accolade of being Europe's most bombed hotel. And I have to admit that for the first time in my life I did read the fire instructions thoroughly and I was none too pleased to discover one night when the fire alarms went off that it was just the rugby club having a bit of fun. The programme was called *The Royle Line*. It didn't have quite the showbiz razzamatazz of *Royle Progress*, but it did take a lighter look at religion, as well as making some serious comment. I acted as an outsider looking in on the religious situation in Ulster.

Shooting the opening title sequences was great fun. It was decided that we would use the same signature tune as *Royle Progress* and that there should be shots of me arriving by air at Aldergrove Airport. They decided to film one of my actual arrivals on a British Midland flight. When the plane taxied to the stand, Andy radioed the pilot and asked him to let the other passengers off first; I was then to come down the steps at the end. As I was just about to leave the plane Andy again radioed the pilot with a message for me: 'Tell him,' he said, 'that if he comes down those steps and kisses the ground, we'll kill him!'

They continued to film as I walked to the arrivals hall; just for fun, as I passed one of the airport officials I flashed my passport at her. She, playing the game, just raised her eyebrows and smiled, but many of the viewers were not prepared to play the same game. The first Monday night when the show was transmitted the telephones kept ringing with people saying, 'Doesn't this idiot know that he doesn't need a passport to get into Ulster?' Humour doesn't always bring a smile to everyone's face.

The programme was never hard-hitting or political; it tried to stay in a lighter vein. I know that I would not have been able to cope with an in-depth analysis of the situation and I think that at times it helps if people know there is a lighter side. The only time I did get near to being involved in the troubles was when we were filming a sequence about a group of people who were raising money for a Roman Catholic parish. The people were training for the first Belfast Marathon, so I went out with them on one of their early morning jogs. With a microphone strapped to me, I interviewed the leader of the pack. The interview sounded a little as though I had a severe attack of asthma. Sport of any sort has never been my line, and as I puffed and panted it certainly showed. I knew that in the band of runners there were two priests, so before I asked the leader if I could have a word with them, I did say, in fun, that I was surprised that he was keeping such company. He laughed, as did the priests, and the interview continued.

When I was in the studio linking the programme together I cued in the piece of film. As they watched, the studio cameramen said that I would never get away with that; I said that I would be very sorry if I couldn't, and fortunately I did.

Once again the programme ran for only one series. I am not quite sure why. I do believe that the religious advisers were not too happy with it and so they were not prepared to press the programme planners to try another series. But for me it was more experience and it helped me to cool down in front of the camera.

At the start of *Royle Progress* I was hyperactive in front of the camera, and when I watched the first programme I was exhausted just seeing myself on screen. You could see the sweat and effort that was going into the performance and it only just remained this side of being OTT – over the top.

This has always been a problem. I am used to live audiences, whether they are church congregations or after-dinner gatherings. With a live audience I do tend to be larger than life, but this doesn't work with television. It becomes far too much for anyone to take.

With both *Royle Progress* and *The Royle Line* at the back of my mind there was a sneaking question which is with me the whole time: was I promoting Jesus or Roger Royle? Many people think it's Roger Royle, and this is why I draw criticism and, in some cases, resentment. Also some people feel that I waste the wonderful opportunities I am given because I am so determined to project my own personality. I realise that I do not find it easy to adopt the John the Baptist role, but I do believe that my personality, as well as my being a man made by circumstances, is also God-given. As I look to Jesus as a teacher, performer and entertainer, I see him as someone who used his personality. His teaching is often hard-hitting and direct, but it is also presented in lighter terms. The point may be just as direct, but the presentation is a lot gentler.

The use that Jesus makes of parables shows that he is prepared to feed with milk as well as with solid food. But I do realise that his teaching was always coupled with his determination to do his Father's will. And it does concern me when I am seen just as a 'media vicar'. However, since I have become a freelance broadcaster I have found it difficult to have my roots planted properly in the Church.

Fortunately there was no gap between *The Royle Line* ending and some new television work appearing. Although by this time Southern had disappeared, the new company, TVS, was prepared to be friendly towards me. Having done the last epilogue for Southern, I did feel a little hypocritical when, the next morning, I was among those people who were saying welcome to TVS, but then that's showbusiness.

The programme I presented was a little fifteen-minute filler at 5.15 on a Wednesday afternoon. It was called *Good News of the Week*. It was a delightful programme to present because it was full of good news stories. It even had a 'Rog'll fix it' element. There was the elderly Hampshire lady who had never been to London; the girl who wanted to have tea at the Ritz with Lulu (she had a pony called Lulu); and the girl who fancied her chances as a weather forecaster.

In this programme there was no thought of going over the top, and my producer Anthony Howard and a researcher, Paul Slater, kept me well supplied with good news. This was also the first television programme I had done in collar and tie, rather than my dog-collar. It proved a very important turning point. There has always been the question both within myself and, I know, in others, of whether I was using the dog-collar as a mere gimmick. Actually, I don't believe that it is a gimmick, because it has always been part of me. I would be naive if I didn't also realise that the dog-collar has opened some doors for me. I hope that I will be regarded as an entertaining after-dinner speaker without the collar, but I do realise that the collar adds something. It is mainly because people have limited and stereotyped ideas of people in dog-collars that I score – people don't expect a man who wears a dog-collar to be funny.

I also realise that the dog-collar has closed doors for me. As I tried to increase my work as a broadcaster people could not see me as anything other than a 'hands together, eyes closed' man. People are very keen to keep their priests within confines. They feel that as long as the clergy are kept within their churches they can do no harm. Generally these are the same people who attack the Church for being out of touch.

All went well with *Good News* until it was decided that it should be amalgamated with all the other fifteen-minute fillers that were being transmitted during the rest of the week. At one time it was thought a good idea to pair us up, then it was decided to join us all together. The next decision that had to be made was when the new, composite programme was to be scheduled and how long it should be. It chopped and changed so much that it is difficult to remember how many different permutations and combinations were produced. In the end it became a half-hour show, broadcast early on a Friday evening and presented by John Junkin, Toni Arthur, Roz Hanby, Lucy Morgan and myself, plus a comedy duo called Burke and Dale. It travelled under the title *The Natives Are Getting Restless*, although I can't remember why. The set was amazing. The five of us were perched on stools on a very high rostrum, looking like Aunt Sallies at a fairground. It did, however, pander to one of my desires: I had a staircase to walk down at the start of the show. But, to say the least, the diet was over-rich and for many people it was just indigestible – though it was great fun to make.

With the death of *The Natives* little other work came my way on the broadcasting front in the south, but Granada, based in Manchester, came to my rescue. I had guested once or twice on a very interesting and relaxed programme presented by Shelley Rhodie and called *Live from Two*. It was transmitted at 2 p.m. and it came from Studio Two. I do remember one time when it wasn't relaxed and that was when I was appearing on the same bill as Victoria Wood and Julie Walters. How I managed to say anything serious at all with them making outrageous comments the whole time I shall never know.

When they decided to move Shelley to later in the evening and rename the programme *Late Night from Two*, they thought it would be a good idea to end the programme with a live epilogue and that I should be asked to do it. I have never experienced anything like it in my life. I was being driven in from all over the country to do before a live audience an epilogue which could last anything from three-and-a-half minutes to about half a minute depending on the time that was left at the end of a programme. Not only Shelley but also the other presenters, Susan Brookes and Bob Greaves, realised I had been given a difficult assignment.

One night I was slightly more involved with the programme. The main guest was Su Pollard of *Hi De Hi* fame and of course the discussion got round, quite naturally, to holiday camps. As I'd been to several holiday camps I was brought in on the discussion. Soon Su, in her marvellous flamboyant and fun way, started running her hand up and down my thigh with the words, 'What a lovely vicar.' I nervously suggested that with this being live television, it might be misinterpreted. After the show, though, she did not let up. We were both staying at the same hotel. As we arrived in the foyer she declared, in that unmistakable voice of hers, 'The vicar won't be needing his room tonight, he's moving in with me.' I hastily explained to the porters that this was not true and made a bee-line for my own bedroom as visions of *News of the World* headlines flashed before my eyes. However, it's the sort of comment that is not easily forgotten, and two years later when

I was again staying in the same hotel the porters reminded me of the incident.

Having finished the programme one Friday night, the producer Trish Kinane suggested that I might take a look at the Boiler House exhibition at the Victoria and Albert Museum before I returned to Manchester on the Tuesday. I would then be able to comment about it on the programme. On Monday afternoon the telephone rang at home – it was Trish. She told me not to bother about the Boiler House, in fact I was not to bother about any more epilogues – I was being dropped from the show. I was assured that it was nothing that I'd said, nor was it because of a poor performance. It was just that they had decided not to continue the spot. Very soon there was a ring at the doorbell. It was Interflora with a plant as a parting present.

I didn't find it easy to accept that I had been dropped and, despite reassurances to the contrary, I went over and over in my mind what I had done wrong. I now realise that it is one of the hazards of the game. It still isn't easy to accept, but you are being totally unrealistic if you think it doesn't happen.

There were two more visits to Granada and on one of them

I actually managed to stand on holy ground – the set of·
Coronation Street. The programme I recorded on my final
visit never saw the light of day, but the first visit was for the
last night of *Late Night from Two*, when we were discussing
the seven deadly sins. Molly Parkin decided that she was
going to add a little sparkle to the programme and began to
attack me and the Christian faith. I hope that I defended both
reasonably well, but I was glad to say that another guest on
the show, Russell Harty, gave his support. But it put me on
my toes. I am not keen on arguments off screen and I certainly
don't like them on. Still, it all ended happily enough in the
Green Room.

After those two shows, no new media work seemed to come
my way. The after-dinner speeches kept me solvent and
meant I still had a roof over my head, and I went back to
part-time teaching at Sherborne School and my old school, St
Edmund's in Canterbury, but having tasted the broadcasting
world I was hungry for more.

There was, however, one other part of the media which had
started to occupy my time and that was the world of *Woman's
Realm*.

11

WHAT I HAVE WRITTEN

While I was working for Save the Children, Wendy Riches, the head of public relations, suggested that I might do a short tour of Poole, Manchester and Cardiff with the then Agony Aunt of *Woman's Realm* Clare Shepherd. *Woman's Realm* had decided to do an appeal to support a nurse in the Sudan and that nurse was Dora.

The idea was that Clare should talk for half an hour about being an Agony Aunt and then I should talk about Dora and her work in the Sudan. I had been fortunate to visit the Sudan even before I went to make the film. I'd acted as a courier on a trip to the Holy Land at Christmas, but instead of travelling back to London with the holidaymakers, I took the next flight into Egypt. I spent New Year's Eve at the pyramids (well I thought it would make a change from Trafalgar Square) and then travelled on to Khartoum. So when I came to speak not

THE PYRAMIDS

only did I know what I was talking about, I also had my own slides of the country to show. One thing I am definitely not is a photographer. Even with an idiot's camera, like mine, photographs seem to have quite a lot of room for improvement.

The tour went well, especially in Cardiff. Old loyalties die hard; my mother's former Guides and my father's former parishioners turned out to support the local lad. After one of these sessions we were having supper and I mentioned to Clare that I would like to write for a women's magazine. I had made the same point to Claire Rayner some time before and she had kindly taken me out to eat at Joe Allen's, off the Strand, and shown me how an article should be set out. I still have the paper napkin on which she drew the plans.

Claire suggested that I write an article of about 750 words and submit it, along with a few ideas for future copy. The first article I did was about my corner shop. Len who ran the shop with his family co-operated well with the research and I called it 'Open All Hours'. I submitted it and was summoned by the head of Features, Anne Wallace, to discuss it. To my surprise not only was Anne willing to buy it but she also wanted me to start a weekly column called 'It Takes All Sorts'. I said yes immediately and travelled home on winged feet.

That evening I bought the *Evening Standard*, saw a flat advertised for sale in the area and in my price range; I went to see it, liked it and bought it. The fee that I was to get from *Woman's Realm* was to help me pay the mortgage.

The demand of writing a weekly column is great: it had to be amusing, so I kept my eyes open for any situation that would translate into 750 words. Open days at sewerage farms, the terror of school assemblies, the sensitive care of my hairdresser, all got the *Woman's Realm* treatment. And with each article went a photograph of me in the situation I was writing about. This took me into the world of the photo-session. Having only been used to holiday snaps, the photo-sessions came as quite a shock. I never knew there was so much to them. Fortunately Ian Tyas, the photographer, knew that I liked to be on the move and so we generally travelled at speed. But not all photographers are prepared to work in such a way and it is important to remember that their art form is just as important as the person who is writing.

News filtered through to me that there was to be a change of editor and that the magazine was to be revamped. I kept my head down and just hoped that everything would carry on as normal. It wasn't long before the new editor, Richard Barber, dropped me a line, thanking me for my contributions to the magazine, but saying that as it was taking on a new shape, my services would no longer be required. Once again, I'd got the sack. I should have got used to it by now, but it still felt like a painful rejection. There have been many times when I have had to be grateful for the belief that God never rejects us.

My last article appeared in the September, but I was asked to do a little piece for Christmas, so at least I felt that the parting had been on friendly terms. The following February I received another letter from Richard Barber. The magazine was celebrating its Silver Jubilee and the readers had been asked what they missed most from their magazine. A lot of them wrote in saying that they were missing me. I think, in all honesty, that more people were missing the Vet, but Richard had the charity to invite me back.

This time my article was to be specifically Christian. It was only to be 150 words, but it had a marvellous place in the magazine on a double page called 'All Around the Realm'. It meant that it was part of the general life of the magazine rather than stuck away in a corner. The only objection I had was that the title 'Thought for the Week' was in Gothic print. Why will editors put religious articles in such special print? My aim has always been to teach that faith is part of ordinary life and not something that has to be set aside in a special container.

Richard moved to *Woman* and the new editor, Judith Hall, summoned me to see her. Once again I thought I was about to be told that my services were no longer required. Instead I was told that my article was to grow: it was to be given a half page. It was still to be an article that had as its basis faith and values, and this time it was to be called 'Royle Mail'.

Obviously there are times when people object to what I

write, but I hope that I write in a non-doctrinaire way which respects both my firmly-based Christian faith and the values and teachings of the other major faiths. I believe that a divide will eventually come between those who believe in God and those who don't, rather than people worrying about what sort of god to believe in. But I do believe that people need to be protected from some of the religious sects that try to manipulate people into submission. For me the Christian faith is there to free people – the gift of forgiveness is the gift of growth – whereas many sects try and instil a guilt which imprisons people.

Women's magazines have a tradition of having a religious column, although it seems that for some years they had dropped the idea. From the letters and comments that I get, it is obvious that many women and even some men – because they do own up to reading the magazine sometimes – enjoy being able to think about their faith as well as their cookery, their knitting and their problems. I would, however, love to know who actually buys the magazine, because a tremendous number of people that I speak to say that they see it at the dentist's, the hairdresser's or the doctor's, and those who admit to reading it in their own homes generally seem to have it passed on to them by someone else.

My association with *Woman's Realm* does not stop at writing a column. It also means a few fun-packed days by the seaside each year. Clare Shepherd started a holiday scheme called 'Find a Friend' – no, it isn't a dating agency! Originally, it was started as a holiday for those people who had recently been widowed or divorced. The idea was tremendous, as many people find holidays on their own rather frightening.

It started at The Devon Coast Country Club, at Paignton in South Devon. You called it a holiday camp at your peril, but it was a series of chalets with a central feeding and entertainment complex. Clare asked if I would like to join them, and I was only too pleased to do so. It is always nice to meet the people you write for, even if it does mean that they can tell you a few home truths to your face.

While Clare was running the holiday it had a slightly formal air to it. There was a top table to which people were invited during their stay, and anything that smacked of *Hi De Hi* was ruled out. This meant that I had to be reasonably careful.

The days were full of outings to such places as Plymouth, Buckfast Abbey, Cockington – all the usuals. The night was spent dancing to Sid Gately – except on Wednesdays, when it was Sid's night off.

Sid was one of the best communicators that I have ever met. He managed to bring total strangers together and helped them to enjoy themselves. He knew exactly who to pick on, who could take his remarks, and those who were rather shy. Every time I entered the ballroom he had a nasty habit of playing 'Onward Christian Soldiers', and it was Sid who introduced me to the excitements of the Slosh, the Alley Cat, the Birdie, and Agadoo.

For me, the dancing was non-stop as men were in short supply. In the main, you had only a vicar or a coach-driver. But many of the dances were party ones, so partners were not needed.

Generally I did not go on the outings, as I needed a few hours in the day to recover from the previous evening. But one Easter day I decided to go. We were heading for Wide-combe in the Moor. Sue, Clare's secretary, decided that she would come as well. We spread ourselves about to try and bring happiness to as many coaches as we could. The coaches left Paignton at 2 p.m. after a marvellous full Sunday lunch. We arrived at Widecombe in about an hour. As soon as the four hundred ladies descended from the coaches, two hundred made a bee-line for the loo, while two hundred made for a cream tea. So Sue looked after the loo brigade, while I looked after the cream teas. As soon as each party had finished, they swapped places. Eventually, with all bodily needs attended to, the whole party went on to see the church and its Easter decorations.

Outside the church there was a group of morris dancers, so we stopped and watched. One of the ladies asked me what the dancing symbolised. Not being too well up on the intricacies of the deeper meanings of morris dancing, I had to confess that all I really knew was that it said something about fertility. With that, one of the ladies gave out a shriek and said, 'Come away Ada, you've had six already!'

It wasn't just fun and games at Find a Friend. Often, in the evening, as an alternative to the dreaded bingo, there would be a discussion or a talk. I remember one night Clare and I were leading a discussion, and somehow it got round to the subject of whether it was worse to be widowed or divorced. The atmosphere got rather strained. I had always had a natural tendency to side with the widows, as I realised how difficult life had been for my mother, but my eyes were opened to the strains faced by those who were divorced. I realised that they too were experiencing bereavement, although it did not have the same social acceptability. I know, however, that some widows would say that they were not regarded as being socially acceptable either.

During my visits to Find a Friend I have also been able to take services. People come, some of whom have not been to any form of worship for some time, and for me it was a privilege to see that their holiday provided spiritual as well as physical refreshment.

When Clare retired and Gill Cox took over as Problem Page editor, she still continued Find a Friend. The style changed, and keeps changing, but I am very glad that I am still included on the guest list. The holiday has moved from Paignton to Warner's Chalet Hotel in Yarmouth on the Isle of Wight, and now many more people from the *Realm* staff spend a day or two with the holidaymakers. But at Find a Friend you can't relax for one minute if you have anything to do with the organisation.

One year some wrestlers had been booked for entertainment. All went well until the last bout and I was asked if I would referee the first round. I realised there would be trouble – and there was. The wrestlers seemed to put more effort into fighting me than each other, but it was all done in great humour. I left the ring fairly shattered, but I did promise to return to referee the last round.

Just before I returned I was warned by one of the bar staff that the wrestlers often started throwing water about as part of their finale. However, they didn't warn me about what happened immediately prior to the last round.

Just as I was returning to the ballroom, where the match was being held, the wrestlers went into another routine. One got the other pinned against a post and then, as he tried to inflict further pain – or what was meant to look like further pain – one of them lost his trunks.

All I could hear as I entered the room were great gasps from the audience and still, to this day, I am not sure whether they were gasps of delight or disgust. But realising that there were some people who would be shocked, I shouted to him to get his trunks back on again, and fast, and I left the ballroom. He did and then finished by apologising for his behaviour and for upsetting the vicar, but said that he couldn't think how such an accident had happened. Little did the ladies know that this had been happening every week for the past thirteen weeks, but his apology took all the steam out of the situation and the happening has now passed into Find a Friend folklore.

One thing I have realised is that the staff of these holiday camps work incredibly hard. The Green Coats at Yarmouth seem to work non-stop, as do those who clean or work in the dining room. The greatest value I feel I offer by being there is just being available for people to talk to me. In the relaxed atmosphere of a holiday it is often easier to try and sort out some of the things that are bothering you. I also enjoy the opportunity that I get to do a double act with Gill Cox. We do a Monday morning talk which, thanks to its popularity, has moved from the Solent Bar into the Ballroom. It is another chance for the Church to be seen as part of the whole of life rather than as an optional extra which you can just think about when you are about to die.

On the corner of my Royle Mail column in the *Realm* is a postmark which tells of the radio show that I present each week on BBC Radio 2, *Good Morning Sunday*. When I became completely freelance I had to keep my eyes open for work. The after-dinner speeches kept coming in and although they are highly paid, and perhaps because they are highly paid, I do find them a great strain. Also, I have only one basic speech, which I adapt, so it is limited in its life-span.

Suddenly London Weekend Television and Thames took a liking to me. With Thames I did a pilot show as a guest on a programme hosted by Bernard Braden. The fact that the show was never broadcast was sad because it was entertaining, but from this I was invited on to a Christmas programme for *Afternoon Plus*, hosted by Mary Parkinson. My fellow guests were Andy Irvine, the Scottish rugger player, Gloria Hunniford and Jimmy Tarbuck. Holding your own against such big names in the entertainment world is not easy, but if you are to be accepted as a clergyman in the media I feel that you have got to be up to their standard. You are often offering something different, but you need to have the same standard of professionalism.

With LWT it was game shows. First *Game for a Laugh*, where one of the hosts was one of my old *Royle Progress* friends, Sarah Kennedy. They had decided to set up a spoof religious programme called *Witness*. No expense had been spared and a very typical, elaborate religious set had been built. There were Gothic arches and stained-glass windows everywhere. The idea was that it should be a discussion programme looking at the state of religion in Britain as we approached the dreaded 1984. An archdeacon, a layman, a bishop and a parish priest were to discuss this weighty subject. To lighten the depth of discussion there was the usual musical interlude supplied by a man on a harmonium and a lady vocalist. The discussion got a little more heated than most religious discussions on television and to crown it all one of the participants spilt some water over the archdeacon. Instead of the usual forgiving and understanding atmosphere that pervades such programmes, a fight broke out. The participants, including the lady vocalist, were, in fact, a team of stunt people. As all hell broke loose the audience watched with open mouths. It ended with the bishop being thrown bodily through the stained-glass window. As the audience wondered what was happening, Jeremy Beadle appeared around a corner and said that we had just been 'Game for a Laugh'.

Tell the Truth I really enjoyed doing. It was a fun game and no prizes were involved. It was the game from which the phrase 'Will the real . . . stand up please' came. Three contestants all claimed to be one person who had something special about him, and it was the job of the panellist to discover which one was telling the truth.

On *Babble* I was an absolute failure. I couldn't even understand the game and things got so desperate at one stage that Barry Cryer said pitifully, 'Oh, let the Vicar win a point.'

All Star Secrets was really another way of presenting a chat show, and you could have no better host than Michael Parkinson. All that happened was that a member of the panel had to decide which other members of the panel had done a particular thing, which was being described in a disguised way by Michael. If that sounds complicated, I can assure you it wasn't. It was trivial and seen as popular Saturday evening entertainment. One critic who found the programme tedious, as well as trivial, thought that the secrets were hardly worth revealing and as for the likes of Fiona Richmond and me being called 'Stars', well then the very word was being devalued. Its greatest value, as far as I was concerned, was working with delightful people, Roy Kinnear and Faith Brown being two of them. It also gave me the opportunity to appear in the pantomime at the New Theatre, Cardiff.

Roy was kind enough to make a personal appearance for me to help raise some money for St Botolph's, Aldgate. Tremendous demands are made on well-known people like Roy who are paid nothing and often have to make their own way to and from the event.

My two appearances on *Call My Bluff* put me on a slightly higher plane. People who thought I was cheapening my calling by appearing on such games as *All Star Secrets* were proud to think that I was on *Call My Bluff*. I actually don't see the difference. *Call My Bluff* is a delightful programme to take part in. I was on Arthur Marshall's side, and he doesn't really worry whether he wins or loses, although he does like to win now and again, if only to please his friends and neighbours in his home village in Devon. I had heard of none of the words and so I was given guidelines as to what to say. The hardest job was to learn the definitions and make them sound convincing so that you could fool the highly intellectual minds of people like Frank Muir. I am not sure whether it is a good thing for a priest to be seen lying deliberately, but the whole evening couldn't have been more enjoyable. When it came to my turn to decide which was the correct definition, it was sheer guesswork. It was no good looking at the opposing panel's faces, hoping that they would give something away. They were all such good actors that even the odd hoped-for hint was not forthcoming.

All these appearances were transitory. No long-running contract was in sight from any television company until just before Christmas, when the *Daily Mail* did an article on Rabbi Lionel Blue and myself. It was on the subject of humour and it was the first time I had met Lionel, but I am pleased to say that that meeting has led to a friendship. Clare Stride, the researcher on the BBC programme *Pebble Mill at One*, read the article and arranged for the two of us to appear on the programme. The atmosphere in the *Pebble Mill at One* studio was one of the best I have experienced anywhere. It was friendly and positive, if at times a little frantic.

The interview went well and during the conversation in 'hospitality' afterwards I mentioned to Clare that I would love to do a series of interviews with people who had overcome problems. We so often wallow in the misfortune of others that I thought it would be good if we could hear of some success stories for a change. I don't believe that good news won't sell. The newspapers are so determined to give us bad news that we don't get the opportunity to taste anything good.

Pebble Mill decided to buy the idea, and once a fortnight, for two series, I interviewed people who had overcome difficulties. My first guest was Sue Arnold, the journalist on *The Observer*. I had noticed that she had written in her column about the time when she suddenly discovered she had a brain tumour. As well as being a journalist, she's a busy mother with a large family. The way she coped with the illness, and the support she received from her family and friends, made a very interesting and encouraging interview.

So did the interview with Janet Taylor, the Yorkshire Dales postmistress who had written a book about the death of her sixteen-year-old daughter, Bridgie. What could have been an extremely harrowing nine minutes turned out to be one of the most strengthening broadcasts I have ever done. In this case it wasn't just a matter of hearing how a family coped, it seemed as though a whole village community had taken Bridgie to their hearts. In addition the interview wasn't short of practical advice to people who found themselves in similar circumstances.

One of the series' most delightful interviews was with Kathy Hebden, a twenty-four-year-old Down's syndrome woman. She had been written off by the professionals who assessed her in childhood as impossible to educate. Nevertheless, she became the first person with this handicap to win the Duke of Edinburgh's Gold Award, competing against people with 'normal' levels of ability.

The interview was live, so I arrived early at the studio in order to get to know Kathy, and Kathy to know me. We built up a trust and a confidence in each other so that when the time came to go on air we were as relaxed as we possibly could be. By this time I knew Kathy's story inside out, so for the start of the interview I could supply both questions and answers until Kathy felt more confident. I think the achievement that thrilled her most was the organisation and execution of the compulsory expedition, and she was only too pleased to display her logbook. Although Kathy said little, the director had the very good sense to keep a camera trained on her the whole time. The warmth of the smile on her face said more than any words.

It was good that Kathy was supported by her mother, Joan, as it showed that this sort of achievement needs to be a team effort.

Among the others I interviewed was a lady with epilepsy.

There is so much ignorance about people who suffer from this illness that it was good, for once, to put the record straight.

As you can imagine, these interviews produced a large postbag. People wanted to express their support or share their problems. Others wanted advice. With the help of Eileen, a very co-operative secretary at Pebble Mill, I did my best to reply. It was good to have a chance to exercise a pastoral ministry again but, being realistic, a letter is in no way a substitute for a face to face meeting. However, the parish priest in me was glad to be able to offer something.

12

TAKE MY YOKE

Living by faith and trust is central to the teaching of the Christian gospel. By wanting to work in the media I was putting this to the test. As a parish priest or a school chaplain I was able to preach this from a position of total material security. I was issued with a home and certainly, as a bachelor, I found my salary perfectly adequate. But now I was forced to practise what I preached – and it has not been easy.

It is quite true that you are only as good as your last performance. It only needs an after-dinner speech to be poor and the news travels along the grapevine at tremendous speed. At contract renewal time there is that uneasy question, 'Will I be re-booked?' As a parish priest I knew that people were not judging me simply as regards my sermons, they took into account my other work: my visiting, the way I conducted the services, my availability. As a performer it is only the performance that counts. The financial rewards may be greater, but it does mean that I am living on a knife edge.

Time and again I have preached that it is only the approval of God that we should seek but, again, as a performer you became hyper-sensitive to the judgments of other people. And I, personally, find it very difficult indeed to separate someone's judgment of me as a performer from their judgment of me as a person. For me, the person is the performer and if you criticise the one then you automatically criticise the other.

As a performer you call for a reaction from people. There are of course a great number of people who will love what you do, and so love you. There will also be a strong contingent who find you insufferable and who are only too prepared to say so. I have had to defend myself more as a priest/performer than I ever had to do as a parish priest. Recently I received an amazing letter from a fellow Christian. He wrote, 'The way you persistently refused to even try and say the Tongan names was demeaning and ethnocentric.' This was because, on a *Songs of Praise* programme, I had had difficulty in pronouncing certain Tongan names. What I was doing was pointing out my weaknesses rather than making any comment whatsoever about the Tongan name itself. However, the writer claimed that, as a Christian, I had a duty to set an example to my fellow citizens. People also have a habit of hearing what they want to hear and attacking what they think they hear. It is quite true that if you can't stand the heat, you should get out of the kitchen. But there are times when I have been caught out by heat being generated in the most unexpected places.

I was shopping for some new dog-collars in the ecclesiastical outfitters, Wippell's – not an exceptional thing for a clergyman to be doing. Suddenly I heard a voice from across the floor of the shop, 'I expect he's paying for those out of his television fees.' It amazed me that anyone could make such a comment. But I have become very aware that being in the public eye not only creates love and hate, it also creates jealousy. I am especially saddened when this comes from fellow Christians.

Certainly, the feelings of insecurity receded when John Forrest asked me to stand in for Paul McDowell on the BBC Radio 2 programme *Good Morning Sunday*. It was, however, a testing time. I knew that others were also being tried out and I wasn't sure whether it would lead to anything or not. I realised that I hadn't been a total failure when I was asked to have another go when Paul was away again, but the one thing I did learn was that radio and television are two entirely separate entities and need very different skills.

The guest on the second *Good Morning Sunday* that I presented was the Bishop of Chester. I travelled up to Chester with John in the car and he mentioned that he was sad that Gerald Priestland was giving up presenting *Priestland's Postbag* on Radio 2's *Pause for Thought*. He'd been answering questions raised in listeners' letters. 'Why don't you let me take over the spot,' I suggested (no immediate response), 'and we could call it *Royle Mail*.' John was prepared to buy that, and so started a regular contact with Radio 2.

It was just before Easter 1985 that the contact grew stronger. About three weeks before Easter, Hugh Faupel telephoned me to see if I would be free at Eastertime. 'Well, I had planned to go to Australia,' I replied, 'but if it's something important I can change my plans.' Hugh at that stage was unable to tell me more, but from the little he said I felt that something exciting could be in the air. Hugh had telephoned on the Monday and he thought I should know something definite by the Friday. A week may be a long time in politics, but it is eternity when you are waiting to hear news about a possible job from the BBC.

On the Friday, John Forrest was on the telephone. Could I get in to see David Winter at four o'clock that afternoon? Of course I could, and I was very glad I did. David told me that Paul was leaving *Good Morning Sunday* and asked if I would like to take it over. It was the one programme that I had always wanted to present, so I was thrilled. There was just one more thing though: could I start in two weeks' time on Easter Day, and would I mind doing the programme from a nunnery in Seville? The answer to the first question was yes, and I certainly had no objections to being in a nunnery in Seville. Having committed myself I then set about sorting out the details, but not before John had invited me into his office for a celebratory drink.

Australia had to be postponed and friends telephoned, but I knew that for the next thirteen weeks Sunday mornings from 7.30 to 9 were booked.

Seville is fascinating, especially in Holy Week. Great processions make their way through the streets, carrying symbols of the Passion, statues and religious tableaux. Some of the processions seemed to have a carnival atmosphere to them, while others were in total silence. All this had to be captured for radio for Easter morning.

It was also decided to begin the programme with me in a

horse-drawn carriage, describing the scene and giving the menu for what was coming up in the programme. The driver spoke no English and I speak no Spanish, but we did manage to convey to him that at a certain point, when I looked at him and nodded my head, he would say 'Si'. My nervousness seemed to develop a somewhat serious headshake, so 'Si' came out at very regular intervals, much to the delight of the production staff, who thought that they were working with Manuel at *Fawlty Towers*.

I found the strain of presenting a live programme, especially one coming over a thousand miles from base, very demanding. In one ear I could hear London and in the other Seville. I had no idea of the technicalities of the operation, but certainly Jordi Morrell, the BBC engineer, made everything as easy as he possibly could for me, and I shall always be grateful to his family for looking after me so well when I wasn't working.

The most tense moment of the whole programme was when I thought the mother superior was not going to turn up to do her piece – fortunately she did, though only just in time. At the end of the programme I felt as though I had done a week's work, and there was a certain feeling of giddiness from ninety minutes of pure concentration.

I joined the nuns for my Easter Communion and the remainder of the day was spent 'at rest in Seville', as the holiday brochures would put it. It was just as well that I had some rest, because on my return to Britain I had to record a programme for the following Sunday, record an interview with Malcolm Muggeridge, and set off for Los Angeles.

Long before I joined the programme, plans had been made to stock-pile a number of interviews with American Christians. I find the American religious media scene confusing. The power of some American evangelists is tremendous and there are times when I wonder if showbiz razzmatazz takes precedence over the preaching of the gospel. Fountains which change colour and whose jets are co-ordinated with the hymn tunes say little to me of Jesus Christ. Their teaching is direct, but it seems to be geared to success – and often material success at that – whereas for me the strength of the gospel is the overcoming of failure. There also seems to be little understanding of those with doubts; it is often a matter of accepting a package deal – or else.

Many of the American showbiz stars who are committed Christians are very willing to talk about their faith. The first interview was in Pasadena with William Christopher who plays Father Malachy in the television series MASH. I was at a loss to know what to ask, as I'd never watched the programme, but some carefully prepared notes by my researcher, Judith Peers, gave me enough material from which to work.

With Pat Boone there was no such problem, 'April Love' and 'Love Letters in the Sand' had been part of my own record collection. The Boone house is very welcoming, but very busy. Pat was due to leave that evening for Australia. He was recording two of his own radio shows for transmission while he was away and just before I was due to start the interview we received a message from David Soul of *Starsky and Hutch* saying, 'Come now, or never.' Pat couldn't have been more understanding and he said he could come back later. There then followed what I can only describe as a *Starsky and Hutch* car ride to get to David. Nervous and exhausted, I arrived, and from this tough character (both on and off screen) I got a fascinating interview about his faith and his involvement in social issues.

I was even more exhausted when I interviewed singing star John Denver. We had flown the Red Eye Special through the night from Los Angeles to New York, and there was very little time to freshen up before we had to get to John's hotel. His beliefs are not conventional. His love of nature and things natural give him a belief in the supernatural but not in an organised religion.

During my stay in LA I met Mary Dore. She had her own television show, but her main claim to fame is as the orginator of the Angel Awards – a sort of religious Oscar for excellence within the media. Through meeting her I was invited to be one of the four presenters at the award ceremony the following year. I accepted; appearing live at Hollywood's Coconut Grove was too good an offer to miss. The occasion lacked none of the Hollywood sparkle. The guests of honour were their majesties, the King and Queen of Tonga. Laser beams played on the front of the hotel and robotic angels greeted you in the foyer – and everyone was a beautiful person. I was the third presenter, and for the first time in my life I used cue cards – or idiot boards – as any chance of learning a script was totally out of the question. The people operating the cue cards were brilliant. They were even able to keep up with me when I deviated from the script for either theological reasons or reasons of integrity. But despite the glitter I have to admit that I was pleased when my name was suddenly announced as a winner for *Good Morning Sunday* – I even remembered to thank all the right people in my speech.

The Angel Awards coincided with my next visit to Hollywood a year later. The success of the first interview-collecting visit had encouraged the producers to try again. This time we came back with an even bigger bag of celebrities. The singer Donna Summer, *Dallas* star Charlene Tilton, *Dynasty* star Jack Coleman and Mr T of *The A-Team*, were all willing to give me an interview, although in the case of Mr T it had to be grabbed. The greatest privilege was meeting Corretta Scott King, the widow of the Civil Rights campaigner Martin Luther King Jr, a most gracious lady. Those who came to hear her at Princeton in New Jersey obviously had a great respect for her. She was determined that the dream of her husband was not going to die with his assassination.

Thanks to good research and imaginative production *Good Morning Sunday* has grown. Many people in Britain have been willing to talk to me about their faith: from royalty and stars of stage and screen to people who ring bells in a Devon church, farm in Gloucester, fish in Whitby, holiday in Bournemouth or the Isle of Wight, or hold synods in York.

Having started in Seville, I think my most memorable *Good Morning Sunday* was broadcasting live on Christmas Day from a home for handicapped children in Bethlehem. Their feelings of love and happiness overcame the language barrier, and the joy in the eyes of the modern children of Bethlehem reflected brilliantly the joy given to the shepherds by the birth of that other most special child of Bethlehem.

As I got used to radio I got to like it more and more as a form of communication. I also realised how people concentrated so much more on what is said on radio than on what they hear on television. Over the weeks, the months, the years, letters have poured in and, once again, one of the most important sides of *Good Morning Sunday* is responding to those letters. Thanks to Daph, who types the replies for me, I am able to respond in some way to the needs of those who take the trouble to write. Many of the letters are just for dedications for friends. I should think *Good Morning Sunday* celebrates more ruby weddings than any other programme on the radio. But some of the other letters are less happy.

As a broadcaster I have become the Sunday morning friend of many people who live on their own and this is, obviously, a tremendous responsibility. I also have to respond to problems raised by people who feel that they have no one else to talk to, but it seems to be a great pity that they have to turn to someone who is, in fact, a stranger. In some cases I have tried to link people with their local community, but this isn't always possible. However, with modern technology, I think it is important that the church realises that it can't just care for people on a parish basis; it has to care for them wherever they may be, and wherever they are willing to listen.

With more experience of radio, even the terrifying responsibility of not crashing the pips at eight o'clock has become less of a torment. With television, however, the torment remains.

While I was working on *Pebble Mill at One* enquiries were made by *Songs of Praise* as to whether I would be a suitable presenter for that fine programme. I am not quite sure what answer they were given, but I was invited to do a trial piece about the Jehovah's Witnesses. My director was Valetta Stallabrass. It went quite well and I got a glimpse into the difficulties of learning pieces of script and saying them direct to the camera – it was not easy and I still dread it. But it does mean that having now presented quite a number of *Songs of Praise* I have become a walking guidebook. Places like Worcester, Holmfirth, Tonga, Coventry, Crieff, Larne, Denbigh, Kenya, and Maidstone Prison no longer need a guidebook, you can just come and ask me.

Obviously I passed the test, so I was invited to join Liz Gort in Eastbourne for my first *Songs of Praise Seaside Special*. I was asked not to wear my dog-collar – this didn't bother me, because I know what a barrier it can be. It doesn't worry me whether the audience know I am ordained or not, I just hope that they realise that I 'believe in my heart what I say and sing with my lips', as the vestry prayer puts it. It does, however, worry certain viewers. The questions I get come mainly from church people who sometimes get quite angry that I don't wear the dog-collar.

I was able to share in the hymn-singing at Eastbourne and I try to make sure that I share in it wherever the programme comes from. For me this is very important. It's not always possible, because I can't always fix the extra date in the diary. By being at the hymn-singing, I am saying that I believe in what is being sung and I wish to be part of it and that makes a stronger statement than just wearing a dog-collar.

However, the recording of the hymns can be an ordeal. As you sing 'Abide with Me' for the fifth time, you begin to wonder whether it's all worth while. The reasons for the retakes are nearly as numerous as pebbles on the sea shore: someone may have stared at the camera, the congregation may have overtaken the choir, someone was yawning just as the camera was on him, the sound was lost, or, to use a technical phrase, one of the cameras went down – whatever that may mean. They are all good reasons why it should be done just one more time.

When I attend the recording of the hymns I try to keep the congregation happy between the takes. Smiling faces are more acceptable to the viewer at home than frowning ones. This is much easier when the recording is out of doors, even if it's in the pouring rain, as it was in Coventry recently. But it's exhausting work, rather like doing three hours' cabaret with

the odd break for a song. When the recording is made in a church then I have to be more careful and sometimes this is anything but easy, unless I am in Northern Ireland and the conductor is Havelock Nelson (we make quite a good double-act).

There were complaints by some people about the way I kept the people happy for the Southwark Diocesan *Songs of Praise*, but then I have to admit that I was near the edge. I was reminiscing in a fairly unrestrained way about my days at the cathedral.

On these occasions my key link person is the floor manager. They link the huge BBC vans in which sits the director, the secretaries, the vision mixers – in fact all the important people – with the people who will actually be seen on screen. Floor managers are vital, and when they are the calibre of the two I have worked with in Trafalgar Square and the ruins of Coventry Cathedral, then life is a lot easier. They seem to know exactly how to shut me up so that the recording can continue. The same is true of many of the sympathetic conductors that I have worked with.

The congregations are remarkably patient. It's amazing that some of them don't pack up and go home – but they don't. Even Brownies on a chilly summer night on Brighton beach were prepared to stay with us until the end.

One group of people who do benefit from a visit of *Songs of Praise* to a town are the hairdressers, followed quickly by the florists. There is hardly a hair out of place and the flowers add to the splendour of whatever building we are in. Often there is more 'oasis' in some churches than there is in the Sahara desert!

The most important part of *Songs of Praise* is the interviews. These stop the programme from being what I call 'duvet religion', something you just snuggle up to and think, 'Oh, that's warm, how lovely' but which offers no challenge whatsoever. It has been a great privilege to meet many of the people that I have interviewed. Sometimes I worry if we are just exploiting people's powerful and personal experiences for the purposes of entertainment, or the stirring of other people's emotions. Once when I did feel this was happening I got very angry, but I have to admit it is a very fine balance to achieve.

The main credit for the interviews must go to people like Kerena, Valetta and Chris – and the other researchers. They seem to be able to find the most remarkable people and get from them the stories which have enormous strength. I have never been given a duff story and, considering the number of interviews that I have done, that is some achievement.

Some of the people I have met stick in the mind more than others, but even the saddest story has joy and happiness somewhere within it. One occasion I shall never forget was just before Christmas when I was doing an interview with one of the music masters at Worcester College for the Blind. He himself was blind and it was decided to film him with his choir, a group of about fourteen youngsters, all blind. As they sang, their fingers gently touched the braille so that they could read the words. One lad got his huge braille sheets into a terrible muddle and the girl next to him couldn't have been more helpful as she gave him space to sort himself out. I wasn't quite sure whether this sort of thing would happen in a sighted choir. As I listened to their singing and watched their fingers moving my eyes were full of tears, but the problem was mine. These youngsters were coping with their blindness, I was the one who wasn't.

I have no difficulty in remembering my final question of any interview: 'And what hymn have you chosen for us?' Normally this goes very smoothly. You see a sign of relief on the interviewee's face as they realise that they have come to the end of their ordeal. Little do they realise that this may be nowhere near the end. There can be supplementary questions, as well as 'two shots' and the dreaded 'noddies', still to come. Noddies are reaction shots which are made after the interview has been recorded and there is no easy way to make them look genuine. With one lady, though, the question caused difficulties. She couldn't for the life of her remember which hymn she had chosen. But then, in fairness to her, I don't think she had actually chosen it; instead, as sometimes happens, she was given it.

The choosing of the places, or the people, for *Songs of Praise*, has nothing to do with me, I just go where I'm sent. But it does mean that I have been able to see parts of Britain that I have never seen before and I can rival Egon Ronay for my hints on where to stay, the quality of the food, the comfort of the bed, and the noise of the water pipes.

One of the things that I have learnt, especially from television, is the need for team work. As a clergyman, it is very easy to work as a one-man band. As a television presenter, this is impossible. Led by Stephen Whittle the *Songs of Praise* production team is very strong. With bases in Belfast, Edinburgh, Cardiff, Manchester, Birmingham and Bristol as well as London. I find myself working with very talented but highly different people. Adapting to their skills and demands can be difficult, but in the end it is always rewarding. The essential thing is that all work together; and you would be surprised how many people are needed to bring a thirty-five-minute programme to the screen. I may never understand the intricacies of the technical side of television, but I do appreciate it can be used, especially on those occasions when it links together Christians 13,000 miles apart.

Over the past few years I have been fortunate. I have not been short of work; if anything there has been too much, because alongside the radio, television and writing there have been sermons, speeches, prize givings, openings and appearances. At times I have overstretched myself, which means that not only I but also those around me have suffered.

There is however one regret. I am not quite sure that the Church knows how to use me. I am not short of invitations to celebratory knees-ups but when it comes to basic thinking on how the Church can spread the Gospel, or use some of today's modern techniques, I am rarely used. Possibly I project too much of the lighter side of life. But as God was prepared to become man in Jesus, my faith although pointing to things spiritual is very much concerned with what is going on here and now.

At times the Church, as a human organisation, drives me up the wall, and I am sure the same is true in reverse, but I have always felt the need of the Church's support. It is a little draughty being out front and if nothing else, I could really benefit from their protection.

Still, as my faith has deepened, I can certainly echo the words of the Psalmist, God is my health and strength: a very present help in trouble – and, I would add, also in joy.